MW00907737

HOBART HANDBOOK

on

Edited by
Aaron Burch & Jensen Beach

HOBART HANDBOOKS
a division of HOBART Publishing
PO Box 1658
Ann Arbor, MI 48106
www.hobartpulp.com/books

Copyright © 2015 HOBART HANDBOOKS
All rights reserved

ISBN: 978-0-9964949-0-8

Printed in the United States of America

Acknowledgements:
All works included were originally published on www.HOBARTpulp.com.
An earlier version of "Baseball Messiah" was originally published by *American Journal of Print* in 2001; "Seventh Inning Stretch" by Alice Lowe was republished by *Stymie* in 2013.

Cover art and "Hobart Handbooks" logo by Andrew Beach.

(Pieces presented in two columns are nonfiction; single column indicates fiction, even if and when names of actual ballplayers are used.)

Inside text set in Chaparral Pro

INTRODUCTION

Because I procrastinated, I am writing this Intro the day before I'm to send the completed book files to the printer. But it also means, coincidentally, I am writing it only a few days after going to my first baseball game in a couple of years. I'm not sure how that happened, how those seasons and years passed me by. I've never been the most regular attendant, but I've almost always found the time to go to a game or two every season. Like at least a couple of the contributors mention in their back-of-this-book author notes, you get older, priorities change, years pass. Life happens.

* * *

In 2003, *Hobart* was only a year and a half old, and I was still scrambling until the last day of every month to put together an issue of the website for the coming month. At some point in March of that year, I realized how excited I was for the approaching baseball season, and how many of the writers I knew were also baseball fans. I had the idea that this excitement should be represented on the site, so I emailed a few friends, asked if they had any baseball-related short stories or essays that they would let me publish, or if they might be interested in trying to write something in the next week or two. Nearly everyone responded with similar enthusiasm, and thus was the birth of our annual baseball issue, every April. Of course, there was no idea of it being an annual tradition at the time. There was certainly no idea *Hobart* would still exist twelve years later.

It's become fun, and an honor, to every year hear people say that they look forward to our baseball issue as much as Spring Training, that *Hobart* is as much a part of their Spring as the return of baseball itself. I've tried, over the years, to explain "why baseball." Because of its literary history, I'd propose. Because it is the most narrative sport, because it has the greatest opportunity for metaphor. But, really, it's just because I like it. I grew up playing catch and backyard homerun derby, collecting baseball cards, going to games with my dad.

That's always been the most fun aspect of *Hobart*—having an idea and following it through. Because... why not? It rarely mattered how silly or goofy seeming the idea, and we never really put any consideration into if readers might share our enthusiasms. What mattered was that we found the idea interesting, fun...it excited us. It turns out, if you follow where your excitement takes you, others will probably follow. And so, that's become something of a mission statement, for our journal that never had much interest in mission statements.

* * *

We've had the idea and wanted to do some kind of "best of our online baseball issues" for years, and here is one iteration of that book. We've been doing it for so long (this year is our 13th!), we have too many favorites, so we made some arbitrary rules. Though we've been foremost devoted to fiction as a journal over the years, we found ourselves pulled toward some of the baseball creative nonfiction we've published, and the fiction that felt like, or played with, nonfiction. Stories about Dock Ellis' famous LSD no-hitter, Herb Washington as the only "designated runner" in MLB history, Jim Joyce and his blown call that cost the Detroit Tigers' Andres Gallaraga a perfect game.

* * *

That baseball game a few days ago was an afternoon weekday game. Sunny, blue skies, 72 degrees. Detroit Tigers vs. Oakland A's. It was a beautiful day, but a rough outing for Detroit—they were down 3-0 in the 2nd, and Yeonis Cespedes was taken out of the game for "flu-like symptoms," replaced in leftfield by Daniel Fields, making his major league debut. Only a couple innings later, Fields let a groundball single get by him, an error that let a couple runners score in his first game as a major league baseball player. OAK 6 – DET 0.

Down 7-1 in the bottom of the ninth, half of the stadium already empying out, Fields started a rally with a double. Kinsler singled him home, J.D. Martinez hit another single, and Tyler Collins hit a homerun. The game seemed out of reach only moments earlier, and now Detroit was down by only two.

The rally died there, the Tigers losing their seventh straight, but it still felt special. We witnessed someone hit their first ever major league base hit, and because of the magic of baseball, and the dependence on outs instead of time limit, anything seemed possible. And what better way to think of literature, as anything being possible.

As Claire Zulkey writes in her author note—and because of the coincidence of book layout and alphabet, they are the last words in this book—"Hope still springs eternal."

—Aaron Burch
Michigan, June, 2015

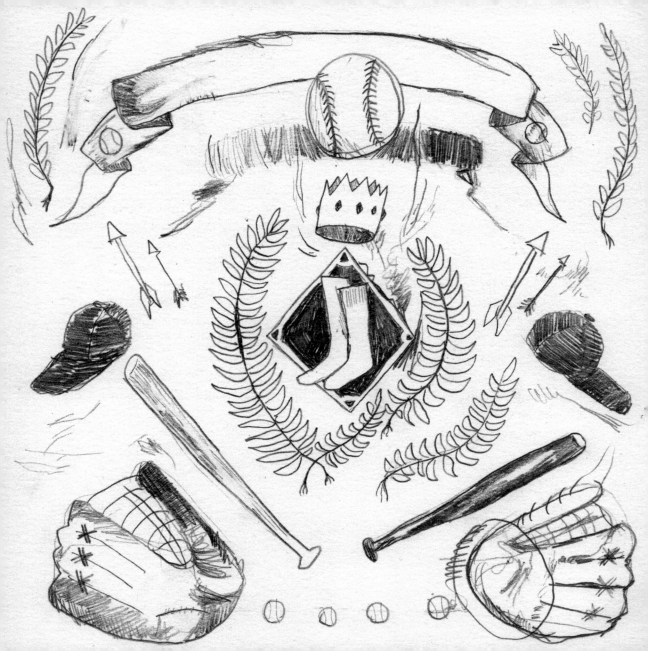

April 1, 2003 | *BASEBALL, Nonfiction*

TAKE ME OUT
Claire Zulkey

Nick Francis Potter

As I write, baseball season is only days away, and I'm so excited. Why? Because my life is empty without it.

Oh, sure, I've got a boyfriend, family, friends, hobbies, work, but what does that all add up to when you don't have a sport to follow? Pretty much nothing.

What about other sports? At the risk of being branded a bad fan, I have a hard time paying attention to games other than baseball if my team isn't doing well, and, as a Chicagoan, it's been a pretty crummy year. The Bears stank it up, the Bulls were typically miserable and the Black Hawks were mediocre (or, at least, I think they were; this matter is complicated by my near total lack of knowledge of hockey.) Same thing with college sports. My alma mater, Georgetown University, developed a specialized talent this season for blowing games in overtime. So basically, I haven't paid any attention to sports since the second or third game in regulation football season.

But thank god for baseball, where for me, spring always brings promise. I'm a Chicago White Sox fan, you see, and recently the Sox have perpetually begun seasons with a tantalizing promise of greatness. Of course, it hasn't added up to much and it brings much frustration, but with spring comes rebirth and hopefully that will come for my beloved Pale Hose.

Following baseball is the ultimate great distraction. Games

1

are played nearly every day, so you don't have that annoying down time that you experience during football season. Plus, not only is your team playing but so are all the others, so that even if the Sox have the day off, I can still follow their rivals to see if they influence the Sox's standings.

Tuning into baseball is like following the news, only not (quite) as depressing; it can be boring or fascinating, painful or joyous. I enjoy listening to games on the radio, because it feels more old-fashioned and it's more exciting to hear the announcers interrupt their hokey jokes and corny asides with frantic descriptions of close plays and home runs.

And, in the end, you feel for your team. If you lose, you're depressed or frustrated or angry, and if you win, you experience a misplaced sense of accomplishment as if you were playing the game along with them. Even though you know it's foolish and it's only a game, you feel it anyway.

This is the escape. This is what I'm waiting for. Hope springs eternal, not just in baseball but in life, and that's why I'm excited for this spring.

David Kramer

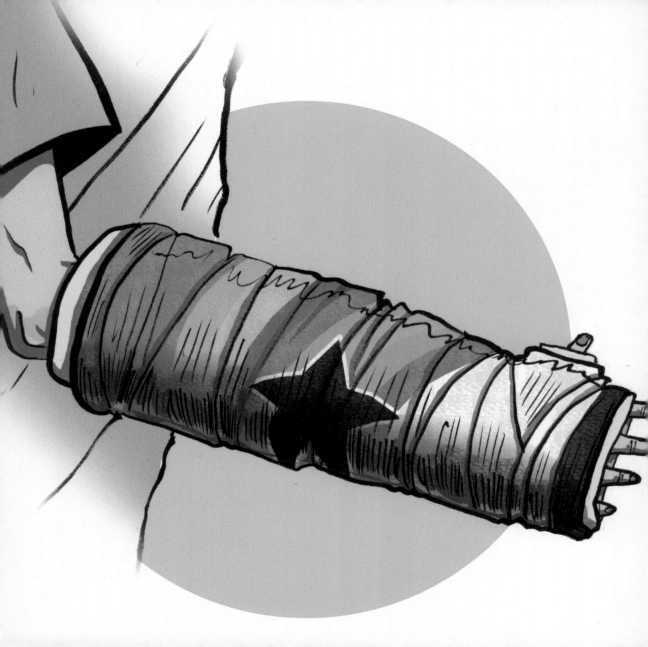

April 1, 2003 | *BASEBALL, Nonfiction*

BASEBALL MESSIAH
Whitney Pastorek

Hard to say where she began, the tomboy in me, but the first sign was surely the way I broke my arm in first grade: I tripped over Allen Marshall while running the bases in kickball. Allen was crouched down, tying his shoe, and I was going full speed on the asphalt. I didn't see him, I saw third base. I would continue to break one of my arms virtually every year of my childhood—as well as almost all of my fingers, my big toe, and both ankles (several times), not to mention incurring numerous head injuries as an aggressive soccer goalie—and by eighth grade, I'd broken so many bones in so many different athletic accidents that when I was pushed into the wall of the gym after a breakaway lay-up, there was no question about the result: my arm is broken, I remember saying, and you need to call my mom. The coaches were reticent, asking, how do you know? Trust me, I thought. I know.

It is perhaps surprising then that my most infamous injury would come during a brief fourth-grade attempt at girlyness. In our backyard in Houston my parents had installed a large playground swing set, heavy green metal poles anchoring three u-shaped swings of black rubber. My sister Lauren and I were expert swingers after years of practice, and our greatest skill was jumping off the swings from incredible heights. One ill-fated spring afternoon, we were outside with a tape player listening to

Samara Pearlstein

5

the soundtrack from Annie, singing along at the top of our lungs; at the tragic moment we were listening, specifically, to "It's a Hard Knock Life." Those unfamiliar with the song should know that it is a brash, inspirational tune about freedom from slavery and breaking the chains that bind us all, even innocent little children. It also has a large, lift-the-cloud-and-belt-it-out type of ending, and it was this ending that inspired both me and Lauren to time our jumps off the swings with the final, "It's. A. Hard. Knock. Liiiiiiiife," landing, arms outstretched, with the last note.

So this is a girly thing, right? Annie is girly, right? See, that was my thought, my terrible, hubris-riddled thought, as I prepped for the leap. I got to "It's. A. Hard. Knock..." and swung back, and looked straight down (for I was parallel to the ground at this point) and I—well, I let go. And I rushed to the earth, straight down right into the fine Texas dust

I had been soaring over the beat before, that dust now in my teeth and up my nose and in my eyes and rocks poking at my legs and where is my arm I can't feel my arm and oh god I can't breathe. My mother, who had been tending to some sort of sickly plant near the house, came running over to see how on earth her baby daughter had managed to cast herself off the swing in such a violent manner, and why wasn't she moving? She rolled me onto my back, took one look at me and yelled, Lauren, get your father, your sister broke her arm again. Sure enough, I looked down at my right hand and it dangled there, marionette-style, at a 90 degree angle to the rest of my arm. Interesting, I thought. Lauren, god bless her, took one look and fainted dead away.

After a dramatic afternoon at the hospital, we learned that my left wrist, very quietly, had been broken as well, and for the first time, I would need two casts instead of just one.

WHITNEY PASTOREK

Oh dear, what a disaster: the two broken arms effectively prevented me from appearing in the recital for my first-ever musical theater class. That was to be my big coming out, you see, my big chance to smile and sing like an angel and show the world once and for all that I was a pretty girl who could wear a pretty dress and sing pretty songs. But it was not to be— the director was adamant that no cripple would perform on his stage, and besides, what if I knocked into one of the pretty girls with my big, monstrous, ugly casts? Heartbroken, I gave up on my last attempt at a girly after-school activity, deciding the fates were against me. As revenge against God for making me a girl, I would learn everything there was to know about the Houston Astros.

In 1962, Major League Baseball welcomed two expansion teams to the National League: the New York Mets and the Colt .45's of Houston, Texas.

In 1975, on the day I was born, the Houston Astros beat the New York Mets, 6-2. If you'll allow me, I would like to propose that the seemingly inconsequential victory of 'Stros over Mets—of Cain over Abel, if you will—sparked something in the Houston Astros franchise. I know this to be true. Hell, maybe it started earlier, maybe it was my first heartbeat as a fetus that started something, but all I know is, on the day I took my first breath in this world, my future converged with that of the former Colt '45s, and I became the Baseball Messiah.

The summer I broke both my arms was 1985. The Astros went 83 and 79 that year, and Nolan Ryan pitched his 4,000th career strikeout. The lineup was solid: a combination of grizzled veterans and fresh-faced rookies who began to play steady ball, championship ball, and they ended the summer in a very respectable third place. And by the end of that summer, during which I lay in bed unable to move, my two casts heavy across my chest, I was a ten-year-old girl who could turn down the sound on the television during games and do the play by play. I listened to a transistor radio under my pillow during night games, through the post-game call-in show, and all the way to the station sign-off. I learned to keep score and memorized stats and read the sports page before my father could get to it, every morning. I was obsessed. I wanted to be the first female major league baseball player, but, failing that, I thought maybe being a sportscaster or a manager or even a ballboy would be ok. I lived and breathed baseball. And whatever my skills are as the Messiah, they carried the Astros through the off-season and into the greatest year in franchise history.

Attendance on Opening Day 1986 was abysmal. But our H-town boys played that season like they'd wandered into some turbo-charged pants, and when it came down to the wire, there were the Astros, in first place. Heavens to Betsy, they were beautiful to behold.

And then.

And then there was the horrid, life-altering 1986 National League Championship Series. Cain vs. Abel. Good vs. Evil. The Houston Astros lost to the New York Mets in the sixth game, perhaps the greatest game of baseball ever played, a 16-inning epic that ended when Kevin Bass struck out—with the winning runs on base.

Sigh.

While it seems pertinent to go deeply into the machinations of the 1986 NLCS, I, well, I can't. It's too hard. Oh, the melodrama, but seriously, people, realize that I was pretty much a shell of a girl after that series. I sobbed. I didn't understand and couldn't get my mind around the concept of a moment—nay, a season—gone. Over. And it would never come back. I had broken two arms at once so that the Houston Astros could have that one shot at greatness, and they'd let me down.

I bought a large, glossy, collector's edition book-thing of the championship-season-that-wasn't-quite, and I read that thing until the staples came out, searching for answers:

Was it the jinx of gaining home-field advantage, even though the Mets were technically supposed to have it? The Astros and Oilers shared the Astrodome in the early fall, and unfortunately, on the Sunday of the NLCS, the Oilers were scheduled for a home game. The only answer was to flip-flop the series schedule, starting in Houston instead of at Shea—totally unfair, I will admit. But my god, who, when scheduling the Astrodome for the fall, would have envisioned the need for playoff games? Why not allow the hapless Oilers to hold a game smack in the middle of the series—no one thought there would be a series. So no, that wasn't the Astros' fault. We'll blame the Oilers for that one.

Was it Game Two, a game the 'Stros flat-out threw away, stranding nine runners on base to lose 5-1? I can't imagine those unused runs were the problem. Maybe the scoreboard—oh, that beautiful scoreboard, with its snorting bulls and lassoing cowboys—was having difficulties. Maybe the organ was broken. Something was clearly a little off.

So perhaps it was the ninth inning of Game Three, when the Mets' Wally Backman bunted, and then ran way the hell out of the baseline to avoid a tag, sparking a rally against the quietly heroic Dave Smith. If he hadn't gotten on base illegally, there's no way anyone hits a two-run homer to win the game. Oh, how these types of things would make me start crying in the middle of math class that fall.

But no, I think it all comes down to Game Six, to the last at-bat of the sixteenth inning... and maybe right down to the fact that in the end, I wasn't enough.

* * *

Last summer, I went to Shea Stadium for the first time in my entire life. The game was Mets vs. Astros, Cain vs—oh, forget it. The Astros lost, all right? I was the only person sitting in Shea wearing a 'Stros hat (circa 1986, none of this modern star crap, I want orange, I want huge), cheering my brains out when they announced the lineup, and then I think the Houston boys went out there and gave up something like 12 runs in the first inning, I mean, it was a bloodbath, plain and simple, maybe the most emphatic win the Mets had this whole season.

But falling behind 12-0 in the first allows one to maybe stop worrying so much about the game and take in one's surroundings, and as I leaned out over the upper tier railing and looked around, I started to have the strange feeling that I'd been here before, in this very ballpark. There were the multi-colored seats:

red, orange, and blue, in honor of the Mets' colors. There was the tacky-yet-wonderful scoreboard paraphernalia: a giant apple that rises out of a hat in honor of home runs. There was the parking lot and highway out past the center field wall. There was the... roundness of it all.

And that's when it hit me: put a lid on this park and Shea becomes the Astrodome. And talk to any one of the fans walking out the gates and they can tell you stories of loss and pain and haplessness that would rival my own—and then come back with a story about how in 1986, they were wearing a Mookie Wilson t-shirt the day he slapped that ball between the legs of Bill Buckner to force a Game Seven and go on to a Mets World Series victory for only the second time in club history and how it was meant to be and they just knew it because they've always felt a special connection with their team...

...and I sort of figured out that my gift isn't really so much of a gift at all, but rather the magic of baseball extended into my life so far that it's become a part of me. And listen, ever since 1993, I've been a Yankee fan. People forget: they were not a very good team in 1993. But when I moved to New York (on Reggie Jackson Day, no less), something changed.

Thus, so long as the Yankees keep winning, I can keep claiming to have something to do with it. I don't think there's anything wrong with that at all. I am the Baseball Messiah.

And wow did the Mets suck last year. Ha ha.

April 1, 2004 | *BASEBALL, Nonfiction*

PRICELESS
Elizabeth Ellen

Halfway there, speeding down I-75S at ninety miles an hour because we're not yet late and I want to keep it that way, I take a peek at her in my rearview mirror. I look at my eight-year old girl, mindlessly singing along with Avril Lavigne because we've just finished listening to Nirvana and so it was her turn to pick, and think how lucky she is. No one ever took me to a baseball game. That's what I'm thinking. You think about these sorts of things a lot once you have a child of your own, about how you got gypped. You think about how maybe you wouldn't have been such a klutz in gym class if someone had just once taken you out back and thrown you a goddamn ball. Which is, of course, exactly why she spent two hours every morning in July at baseball camp this summer and also why we're right now headed to Comerica Park in downtown Detroit on a beautiful Sunday afternoon in late August. Things are going to be different for her. If we ever live in Arizona for a year, you can be sure as shit, she's going to see the goddamn Grand Canyon.

Last night, in anticipation of today, we watched "The Bad News Bears" and "The Bad News Bears Go to Japan," because everything I know about baseball I learned from the movies. But I'm pretty sure all she learned from watching "The Bad News Bears" was how to curse, cause all day today she's been doling out swears like a drunken sailor.

"Mom, I can't find my damn shoes!" "Mom, the asshole cat just puked on my bed again!" But I let her. I figure the novelty will wear off after a day or two anyway, if I don't make a big deal about it. And besides, I'm tired of all the political correctness. I'm tired of moms telling me, "Johnny can't watch Sponge Bob anymore. They use the s-word, you know— stupid, and stupid is a bad word in our household." I tell her it's okay by me if she wants to swear, just make sure Johnny's mom doesn't hear, cause she's retarded; she wouldn't understand.

By now we're in the city, we're just about there. We already passed all the cheap parking lots because I didn't realize how close we were and now that we're right on top of it, it looks like we're going to be shelling out twenty bucks to park. But, hey, at least we're here. We made it. We didn't get lost and it's not raining. It's 75 sunny degrees. Perfect.

We cross the street and fall in line behind twenty-five other families and five Boy Scout troupes. There are kids everywhere. You've never seen so many kids! All of them running and laughing, with their baseball caps and gloves. They don't care that Detroit has lost eleven straight games. And neither do we. That's when I notice the sign. One of the scouts is pointing up at it. Right below "Today: Detroit Tigers Vs. Anaheim Angels" is says "Family Fun Day" in big, red letters.

"Hey," I say, giving her hand a squeeze. "Look, it's Family Fun Day." And I point up at the sign too.

Neither of us knows exactly what this means, but it sounds promising. We shrug our shoulders and smile. We're a family. We like fun. Give us some of that!

The game's already started so we take our time finding our seats. It's a new stadium and there's plenty to see. I don't know if we're in a baseball stadium or Cedar Point, but I swear we just passed a carousel and a Ferris

Wheel. Every few feet there's a glass case filled with Tiger memorabilia, photographs and histories. We stop and look, just in case one of them mentions her great-great grandpa, Bobby Veach. The cases are arranged by decade, and though I've forgotten the exact years he played, I know it was during Ty Cobb's time, so I look for Ty and then look closer to see if I can find anyone who looks like the one picture I've seen of Bobby, hanging on the wall at my in-law's. I think she'll be impressed. Finally, after twenty minutes of searching, I spot a picture of a man who looks like it could be him.

"Hey, look!" I shout, pulling her arm. "I think I found him. I think this might be your great-great grandpa." I point to a group shot from the 1920's. She

presses her nose to the glass and cups her hands around her eyes and sort of squints at the picture, at where I'm pointing.

"Cool," she says, nonplussed. "Now can we get a snow cone? Please"

We get a snow cone. Red. Before the day is over, we will have bought three more: Green, yellow and blue. We will pee a rainbow.

While she shoves overpriced bits of flavored ice into her already reddened mouth, I look for our seats. I look at our tickets, then up at the row numbers, then back down at our tickets. Finally, when it feels like we've walked the entire circumference of the stadium at least three times, and she's complaining that her damn feet hurt and I don't tell her to quit whining because mine are hurting

14

illustrations: Jarod Roselló

too, I find them. The stadium's only half full, but there's a family of giants seated right in front of our assigned seats. We walk back up the stairs and sit in one of the empty rows.

Did I mention neither one of us has ever been to a baseball game before? Neither one of us has ever been to a baseball game before. This is it: our first. And cumulatively we know nothing. Well, not nothing, but close to nothing. Very close. As close as you can get without actually being nothing. Here is what we know: there are two teams, they take turns at bat, three strikes and you're out, three outs and the other teams up, our team sucks. We don't know any of our team's names. In fact, the only baseball players names I do know are Pete Rose (because I went to school in Cincinnati and everyone who has ever lived in Cincinnati knows Pete Rose and Marge Schott), Joe DiMaggio (because he was married

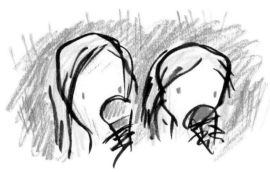

to Marilyn Monroe), and Phil and Joe Niekro (because Joe Niekro was my dad's best friend). There are other names I might know if you said them: the guy Halle Berry was married to for a while, the old guy they made the movie about, but that's about it.

So here we are, at our first baseball game, and neither one of us has a clue what's going on. But we're not about to let that stop us from having fun. We watch the people around us, the ones with their faces painted, the ones with those things that make noise in their hands, the ones with a stack of empties at their feet, and do what they do. If they clap, we clap. If they boo and hiss and make the thumbs down gesture, so do we. And when they try and start a wave, we follow along, despite the fact there is no one on either side of us.

And when all else fails, we buy more food. You know that credit card commercial that shows the father and son at the baseball game and lists the price of everything they bought and then ends by saying something cheesy like: taking your son to the baseball game and having him think you're cool: priceless. Yeah, that one. Well, here is my version:

- Parking: $20
- Tickets: $28
- 4 snow cones, 2 pretzels, 1 popcorn and a bag of peanuts: $23
- Baseball cap you bought because the guy selling them said your daughter looked adorable in it: $18
- Taking your daughter to a baseball game and buying her everything she wants because your parents were hippies and instead of going to baseball games, played croquet and horseshoes in your backyard with their friends while drinking Mint Juleps and eating "adult" brownies: priceless.

It's a close game, but we don't get our hopes up. We root and cheer like our team has a chance, but we know they'll probably lose. And we're okay with that. We keep repeating to ourselves: it's doesn't matter who wins, it's fun just being here together.

Then a crazy thing happens. Just as the game is ending, just as it looks like Detroit has lost their twelfth straight game and the fans are beginning to clear the stands, someone comes on the speaker to announce that after the game, any child who waits in line can run the bases. I look behind us. The line has already begun to form. Luckily, it is

ELIZABETH ELLEN

on our side of the stadium.

"Well, do you wanna?" I ask. "Cuz if you do, we better get in line now."

"Um, okay, sure," she answers, not sounding at all sure, but looking rather excited about the prospect. Her face is all red but I can't tell if it's the snow cone or the sunshine or the excitement.

I take her hand and pull her up the stairs and claim our place in line. It formed quickly, but we aren't too far back. There's maybe twenty, thirty people in front of us. Five minutes later I look behind me and I can't even see the end of the line. There must be over a hundred people in back of us. This has been our luckiest day ever.

* * *

The game isn't officially over, but hardly anyone's paying attention anymore. Most of the people have either left the stadium to go home or are now waiting in line so their kids can run the bases. There's a monitor visible just overhead, and since those of us in line have nothing else to do, we look at it now and then while our kids sit cross-legged on the cement or twirl on the metal bars at the top of the stairs. It's the bottom of the ninth, we're down by one, we've got two outs, one man on base, and our batter has two strikes against him. This looks like it; number twelve. We're all watching now. Something comes over me, maybe the cumulative excitement, maybe wanting our perfect day to be even perfecter, I don't know what it is. I've not a baseball fan, I've never watched a full game of baseball on T.V. Hell, I'm not even from Michigan, but all of a sudden I'm praying for this team to win, praying for a miracle. And just as I'm praying, it happens. We get our miracle. The batter hits that ball so hard and so far I can't even see where it lands. All I know is the other team didn't catch it and our two men are running to home plate. We won! Me and the kid are jumping up and down and high-fiving. We're holding hands and dancing in circles. OUR TEAM WON! OUR TEAM WON! Can you believe it? Did you see it? Everyone's yelling and screaming like our team just won the goddamn World Series.

Before we know it the line's moving and we're following the rest of the people down the stairs and under the stadium. We're moving two by two, one adult per child. Everyone's happy and holding hands and excited. We pass piles of dirt. We pass what looks like farm equipment. We're close now. We can see the field through an opening. That's where the kids have to let go their parent's hand.

"You're going to run the bases with me, right?" she asks, looking at the field with wide eyes. It looks bigger down here.

"No, honey. The kids run the bases and the parents wait for them at the end. You'll be fine. Just follow the kid in front of you."

She doesn't look so sure but before she can back out there's a lady waving her on and a man handing me a coupon for a free kid's meal at Subway. As I follow the parent in front of me I look up at the big screen overhead and I see her. I see my kid, running the bases on T.V., and I can't help but smiling like every other proud parent in front of me.

And then she's back. More high-fives.

"Did you see me? Did you see me on T.V.?" she asks, panting, sweat running down her flushed face.

"I did. You were awesome, baby. I'm so proud of you."

But we don't have too long to stand and bask in her glory. They're really moving the kids around. We're holding things up. I take her hand and pull her up the stairs a final time. On the way to the car we stop at the carousel. They're giving free rides for Family Fun Day. Most of the people have already gone home so there's no line and she gets right on. I stand and watch, wishing I'd thought to bring a camera. A mom next to, who probably has everything in her oversized purse, is snapping away. But then I think there are some moments you don't need documentation to remember. Some moments you just never forget.

On the drive home we go over everything again, recanting every exciting detail like an old, married couple who just won their first Bridge tournament. We don't get many days like this. Some days we fight like cats and dogs. Some days I am "the worst mom ever!" because I'm "ruining [my] life!" But today I'm the "best mom ever" and this is the "best day ever." Because when you're eight years old, there is no gray. When you're eight years old, there is only black and white. And when you're the mother of an eight year old, you take what you can get. And some moments really are priceless.

Jarod Roselló

April 1, 2005 | *BASEBALL, Nonfiction*

Joltin' Joe Has Left and Gone Away
Tod Goldberg

I can't say for certain how much of my father's life was a lie. I know a few things are fact: he worked as newsman for a variety of television stations in the San Francisco Bay Area and the Pacific Northwest. He once won a local Emmy for a documentary he did on stewardesses. He tried – and failed – to produce his own talk show in the 1960s called International Airport; an experience my mother says lead to a nervous breakdown and their eventual divorce in 1973, but that may not be true. I know that my father adopted his own stepdaughter's son and then abandoned the boy as he had his own children some twenty years previous. And I know that my father loved baseball. I know that for the five years I tried to get to know him, before finally deciding on my own that he wasn't a good person, baseball was often the only thing we shared, a kind of filament to a life neither of us had lived.

"Did I ever tell you about the time I played catch with Joe DiMaggio?" he asked. We were sitting in his condo in Rancho Mirage, the last strings of another long fight balled up between us.

"No," I said, "you never did."

"He'd just gotten a job with the A's," he said, "so this was 1968 or 1969, so you'd already been born…"

"No," I said, "I was born in 1971."

"You were? I always thought you

21

were born in '69."

"That's Linda," I said. Linda, at the time, was suing my father to recover hundreds of thousands of dollars in back child support.

"Your sister is an angry person," he said. "You know, I suffered, too. You kids weren't the only victims here."

"I have to go," I said. I'd heard it all before. I'd heard the lies and the truth and in the end I didn't much care to dig out from the divots they both left inside me.

"Don't you want to hear about DiMaggio?"

The fact is that you're always a child to your parents; the truth as it relates to my own father is that he never knew me as a child. Between 1976 and 1995, I'd see my father a handful of times – funerals, a chance meeting at my grandfather's house, my brother's wedding – and in those times we'd talk about nothing in particular, a gulf of anger and sadness filled with ellipses of conversation. And when those silences became too much, when it became clear that genetics alone could not fill in for words, he'd turn to baseball.

"You still a fan of the A's?" he asked me during a lull in his mother's funeral. I was 13 and hadn't seen him in nearly five years.

"Yes," I said. We were sitting beside each other and I could smell his aftershave, a sweet perfumed cologne that seemed all together wrong for the day he'd bury his mother. His tie had been cut in half by the rabbi and I remember wondering if it was an expensive tie, if he'd spent child support money on it, if he was sad to lose the tie, if it was one of his favorites. His face was covered in small bumps of razor burn and I remembered the last time I saw him: he'd come to our house in Walnut Creek and my mother, who raged at the very mention of my father's name in her presence, had kissed him on the cheek, had touched his face with her palm, had told him he needed to shave. It is the only memory I have of tenderness between my parents and I keep it inside me like a yellowed snapshot, until I'm not sure today if that's how it happened at all.

"They're not looking too good this year," he said. "Did I ever tell you I met DiMaggio when he worked for the A's? Played catch with him."

* * *

I'm not a very athletic person. My legs are short and my torso is compact and thick, my arms skinny. The only sport I ever played competitively was soccer and for a time I was good at it, if only by virtue of the fact that I wanted to hurt people when I played. When I stepped onto the field, something in me switched and I became the kind of aggressive person I wasn't in real life – during father/son games, where I was frequently the only son without a father, the coaches had to pull me aside and tell me to dial it down a notch, that I couldn't slide tackle Jeremy Joseph's father. I played for over a dozen years and only scored a handful of goals, but that never mattered. I wanted to drop people. I wanted the players on the other team to be afraid of me; I wanted to be as intimidating as Goose Gossage was on the pitcher's mound, a fat, burly mass of anger that simply did not care about the score, only the one he had to settle.

My father loved Gossage. Or, maybe he didn't, because when you have so few memories of someone, you cast importance on the smallest things, like a visit to a television station in Portland, Oregon where people called your father "boss" and where you two watched a bank of TVs filled with Seattle Mariners highlights, Gossage rearing back and striking out one Mariner after another and your father saying,

"Gossage does it the right way." But it's not your father. It's hardly even mine. You hang onto things when you're young. You control what you can. And maybe, when you play soccer, you imagine you're a baseball player your father admired the last time you can remember seeing him.

* * *

"I'd like you to come to my wedding," my father said. This was in the mid 1990s, my senior year in college, the beginning of a stretch where I would attempt to get to know my father from an adult perspective. My grandfather, my father's own father, had implored me to do it, to decide on my own whether the man I'd vilified in my childhood mind for his abandonment and failure to take responsibility for...anything, simply, anything, was indeed the monster I imagined. Separate from the silences I and my siblings had endured. Separate from the court judgments. Separate from the stories of how he was going to really take care of his adopted son, only to excise him like so much garbage.

"Why?"

"It's time we started acting like father and son," he said. "Your brother is coming."

"That's because you were a father to him," I said. I said it to hurt him, to get a reaction, to drop him. But what made my father incredible, what made the difference between his lies and his truth murky and disturbing, is that he didn't react, never reacted.

"It'll be fun," he said. "We'll even have a little bachelor party." When I didn't respond, because I was somewhere between crying and vomiting, the two poles I typically battled when speaking to my father, he changed the subject. "Your A's aren't doing so well, I see."

"Why do you do that?" I said. "Why do you never address what I'm saying?"

"Because it's the past," he said. "Let's move forward."

The night before his wedding, in a hotel bar in Longview, Washington, while my father's friends tell me what a great man my dad is, how they don't understand why they've never met me or any of my siblings, I watch the reflection of a baseball game in a smoked glass mirror. It's such a simple game. The rules concise. The human contact limited. The chance for redemption as near as the next pitch.

"A toast," my father says, "to my sons," but my brother has long since gone to our room, where, I'll find, he's just as sick as I am.

* * *

I can't remember the last time I saw my father alive. It might have been the time I drove to his house and asked him not to sue my sister, not to force her into bankruptcy, after her attempt to retrieve the child support was thwarted by the courts. It might have been when I drove to his house and asked him not to sue my mother for the same reasons. It might have been another time all together. Scar tissue has formed over many of my memories about my father and when I peel it back, everything rushes together, and I'm nine years old, memorizing the statistics of every major league player, filling my head with numbers and names and all-time records and minutia, anything to stop me from concentrating on what is empty about the rest of my life. By age 12, I know more about Rickey Henderson than I will ever know about my father.

"Your father is a great man," his most recent wife said to me during one of those last visits. "Why you and your brother and sisters can sit around and say such terrible things about him is wonder to me."

"He never paid child support," I said. "I didn't see or hear from him for decades at a time. He was legally not allowed into California because he was such a deadbeat."

"You could have picked up a phone," she said.

"I was 10," I said. I tell her he's doing the same thing to his adopted son.

"Well," she said, "he's adopted. And half black. That was all a big mistake if you ask me."

Later, when his wife had stepped away my dad would tell me how much her son reminded him of me. "You're a lot alike," he said. Her son was the kind of guy who got drunk, ran from the cops and crashed a Camaro into a bank. At the time, my first novel was about to come out and I'd recently married. "But I can't talk to him about baseball like I can talk to you. Did I ever tell you about the time I played catch with Joe DiMaggio?"

* * *

The day after my father dies, I call my mother and ask if she remembers the time Dad played catch with Joe DiMaggio. "What? No, that's crazy," she said. "He never did that."

"He said it was about 1968 or 1969," I said.

"I'd certainly remember that," she said.

We talk for a while about my father, about what he was like long before I was born, about their life together. She tells me I would have liked him then. She tells me he was a good person but that something drove him crazy. She tells me she is sad for the man she married, but not for the man he became. That night, I leaf through old scrapbooks my mother keeps high on a shelf in her house. In these books my father is young and handsome and happy. There are pictures of him with my brother Lee, my sister Karen, my

TOD GOLDBERG

sister Linda, me as a newborn, my mother (who in these pictures is his wife, a notion I cannot imagine), his own long-dead parents, and in each of them I am struck by the sense that I've never known any of these people, at least not in the context of these photos. The more I stare, the more I feel like I'm invading someone else's memories.

And yet, in one of the last pictures, I see a small baby sitting in a high chair wearing an Oakland A's baby-shirt, while a man, who looks so much like me that it snatches my breath, stands in the background, smiling.

April 1, 2005 | *BASEBALL, Nonfiction*

THE WOLFMAN IN BARRY BONDS
Timothy Denevi

Andrew Shuta

I met Barry Bonds once, in person, in contrast to the countless times I've watched him, written about him, looked up his statistics, and heard stories about his high school and college days from over twenty years ago.

I met him just last season. He didn't say a word to me. It was in the San Francisco Giants clubhouse, which, with its wood-paneled lockers, bathroom attendant, and rows of slippers, dress shoes, and shimmering metal cleats, felt more like a posh hotel lobby than a haven for men about to enter a field of grass and mud, emerging afterward with bloody knees and elbows, with eye-black smeared into the rims of their nostrils and strands of chewing tobacco wedged between their teeth.

The clubhouse even smelled immaculate: like mint. A plasma TV looped ESPN footage that occasionally rendered the actions of those present into the realm of High Definition.

My dad and I were with my dad's friend, a former minor-league pitcher who throws batting practice for Barry and who I like to quote in my articles on the Giants: a counter to the negative media perception of Bonds as the proverbial baby-eating steroid ogre.

Everyone in the clubhouse gets one locker, no matter if they earn the major-league minimum of three hundred thousand dollars or upwards of fifteen million. Everyone

29

except Barry. He gets three: a whole corner to himself. He has a Barca Lounger and a nutritionist. He has his own personal TV. When my dad and I entered, Bonds was lounging back, leather footrest propped out, watching this TV. The rest of his teammates were scattered, a foursome of Latin ballplayers laughing and playing cards in their spaceship-slick undershirts, an old relief pitcher, looking overweight without the glamour of his jersey, sitting head down at his locker.

My dad's friend, who'd pulled considerable strings to gain our entry into such exclusive grounds, turned to us quickly and whispered, "I'm not gonna introduce you to Barry. Okay?"

It was about an hour before the game. I stepped lightly, afraid of disturbing some immortal balance between the baseball gods and the hallowed surroundings, worried I could jinx the effort of my favorite sports team, which at the time was fighting for its collective life in a late-summer pennant race. Sports fans, like the devoutly religious, tend to believe that they can somehow manipulate fortunes beyond their control; hence the labyrinthal workings of superstition.

We passed the overweight relief pitcher, and I nodded; a grim smile spread to the corners of his mouth. We detoured around the Latin card players, who continued laughing without a glance in our direction. We had progressed to Barry's corner. My dad's friend stopped. Bonds looked up from his TV, weary. His heavy eyelids, like the rest of his body, seemed to be weighted down by an aggregation of muscle.

"What are you watching?" my Dad's friend said. The words felt parsed, hard chosen. I slunk back, startled by this non-televised vision of Bonds.

Barry's one-word response seemed to flit in and out of the decorous surroundings. It was a moment before I understood what he'd answered: "The Wolfman."

That was it. My dad, standing closer to Barry at the edge of the Barca Lounger, seemed ready to comment back. He had been a minor leaguer himself and was not bound by the same sense of awe. But seeing the slugger's eyes trace somnolent and puffy back to the TV, he said nothing. We left.

I kept thinking—walking out through the dugout and into the grandstand, where autograph seekers parted huffily in the aisle—I kept thinking, What?! Barry Bonds watches clips of a hirsute horror villain before games! Does this somehow gird him for the upcoming at-bats, tickling a predatory response that allows him to become a wolfman of destruction against the cowering pitchers of the National League West?

I vowed to search "Wolfman" on IMDB (which I have since done; a 1979 movie of that name came up, followed by the user comment: "worst acting in film history"). I imagined what a cross between Barry and an evil-fanged wolf-beast might look like (a Doberman with giant forearms, I settled on).

Finally, sitting down the third baseline with my old man, both of us sipping foam from our plastic-cupped beer, I had to ask his take on the whole thing.

"What the hell are you talking about?" he said.

"You know, the movie Barry was watching." I made my fingers into curled claws. "Wolfman."

My dad shook his head as if he were still my little league baseball coach, as if I'd once again missed the bunt or hit-and-run sign. "Look up at the scoreboard, meat."

"Huh?" The Giants were playing Philadelphia that night. Starting for the Phillies was a left-handed pitcher named Randy Wolf. "No way," I said.

"Barry watches clips of every starting pitcher," my dad said. "Jesus.

I think you're the one who told me— it was in one of your columns." He laughed then laughed again. "You thought Barry Bonds, an hour before game time, was watching a horror movie on his private TV set?"

"It seems reasonable," I said.

He sipped his beer, smirking. "No, it doesn't. It doesn't seem reasonable at all."

* * *

After the game—after Barry hit a gorgeous line drive over the right-field wall and into the bay water beyond; after three or four sequels to my original beer—I began to think that it was entirely reasonable. Why not? I thought. The media, the fans, even some of his fellow players all liked to make Barry Bonds into a demon of greatness: enjoying the process of his ascent, hoping he might fall farther than any fall previous.

Why wouldn't Barry also enthrall himself with his own personal monsters? And what better choice than a monster who deep down was nothing but a wild, hairy dog of a man?

Leaving the stadium whipped by the nighttime bay gusts of San Francisco, I imagined a glorious chain of celebrity monsters, each one horrible only in relation to those linked to it; I smiled thinking that somewhere on that chain I—the fanatic fan, hero worshipper, beer guzzler—served a purpose, too.

April 1, 2006 | *BASEBALL, Fiction*

ALL MY CHILDHOOD HEROES PLAYED BALL

Devan Sagliani

She slurps her cherry cola loudly through her novelty straw and winks at me. I'm just turning eleven. She's got candy pink lip-gloss on and a touch of blue eye shadow her older sister helped her smear on. She looks like she's sixteen, but I know she's the same age as me. When she smiles I see the rubber bands on her braces and think about how glad I am that my parents couldn't afford orthodontics.

Even though I am a scrawny white kid from suburbia I pretend I am Reggie Jackson. I'm clutching a baseball that's still sticky from where I left gum on it. I like to wad a pinch of Big League Chew up like real tobacco and stuff it deep back between my cheek and my molar on the left side. I like to spit it like chew, like the ball players do. It's better than sunflower seeds because the salt in them makes your taste buds explode and go numb after a while or the shells get stuck between your teeth.

My Dodgers cap is faded from playing out in the sun

too long. It's covered in dirt from sliding in the red dust at the little league field. This is what freedom feels like when you are eleven, running as fast as you can, riding your bike, swinging for the fences, breaking the rules. Baseball is simple. Baseball is perfect. It's the perfect sport, that's why it's the all American sport. Baseball makes sense in so many ways. It's just nine innings long, which means you get nine chances to win the kind of glory that lasts a lifetime. Baseball is where all my heroes come from.

This is 1982. We are living in a modern age. Israel has stopped Iraq from getting the bomb. There is a lot of hope for the future. The Redwings and the Red Sox just last April played the longest baseball game in history. Reagan's survived being shot by some guy named Hinckley. They shot the Pope last year and the President of Egypt. Seems like everyone is getting shot, but that's not what's keeping me up at night. I'm listening to Duran Duran sing Girls On Film and it's all starting to make sense. I'm changing my sheets more often and having these amazing dreams I can't even begin to describe. More and more I'm finding they have nothing at all to do with baseball.

My great grandfather Julius takes me to all the games at Dodger stadium. Sometimes he takes me out of school and we go during the middle of the day. One time he let me have a sip of his warm beer during the 4th inning and, all the way home, we laughed about the way the concession stand guy yelled out "HOT NUTS". Pappy Julius used to

Jarod Roselló

play for the Sox after the depression, before he broke his pitching arm and went into concrete mixing. He's always got the games on the television with the sound off and the radio going.

He tells me how he rode the rails in a boxcar as a teen, running to catch up with the train. He's full of strange phrases or, as he likes to call it, the Hobo Knowledge. He tells me how he worked all summer to buy his first glove and how much trouble he went to oiling it, wrapping it in a string cocoon with the ball tucked inside to get the shape right while he slept. He tells me about when Castro played ball instead of killed people. He tells me that fruit was like candy back during the depression, that I don't know how lucky I have it. But he means well, he's not mean spirited about it.

She giggles at me, Katie, the candy gloss girl, and I feel hot in the face all of a sudden. She's from a rich family in Westlake. We met at church camp, where she gave me her phone number. When I called her, she said we should meet for a date, but my parents say I'm too young to be dating, so I didn't tell them about it. My dad says there will be plenty of time for dating girls once I'm in high school. Seems like everything is about waiting to be older when you're a kid. All I can think is that I hope I don't run into any of my parent's friends from church. It's bad enough that I ditched out on practice, but being publicly humiliated or grounded would be even worse.

It's a Saturday, my day off from everything, around four. Even though there is still plenty of daylight left, I'm not on the field. I'm sitting across from her not knowing what to say. I can feel the eyes of every adult that passes by us. I'm a wreck, still sweating from hauling ass here on my BMX bike. My Redline with trading cards in the spokes — not the good ones like Fernando Valenzuela or Willie Stargell, but the doubles, and the guys with weak RBI's like the Cub's Ivan DeJesus. My Pappy Julius buys me packs of Topps and I pick up the Fleer cards with my allowance. I spend my nights watching Happy Days reruns or The Muppet Show or Three's Company. I'm starting to understand the deal with Jack Tripper. You can say that it's all coming together, which is why I'm ditching practice and standing looking stupidly at Katie's lip gloss.

Pappy Julius is like a super hero to me. He fought in World War II. He pitched against Jackie Robinson in 1959 during one of the World Series games, a year before he retired from playing ball on account of the accident. He had a picture of himself shaking hands with Dwight Eisenhower dressed in his White Sox uniform and another of him in a business suit with President Richard Nixon, who he calls Tricky Dick with an affectionate smile and a mysterious wink of his eye. He talks about Nixon like some people talk about Santa Claus.

Pappy had a heart attack once while walking home from the grocery, but he thought it was just bad heartburn, so he went back to the store and bought some antacids. He took his time walking back while chewing those chalky mints and clutching his chest. He had to sit down a couple times in the bushes to catch his breath. The next morning when his indigestion still wouldn't go away dad took him to the hospital. Later that day he had a double bypass.

I'm not ready for the onset of puberty. I'm not prepared for acne and having my voice change. I'm not ready for mixed dances, chaperoned dates, and sex ed classes. I don't even have my learner's permit yet.

I'm starting to feel like an idiot staring at her so I sit and she offers me the straw. I take it in my mouth. In my mind I imagine what it will taste like when she kisses me and then the soda hits my lips and squirts out onto my shirt. She giggles as I look up at her while I drink what's left and the straw makes that funny sucking sound against the ice cubes. Then I laugh because I'm nervous. Then she French's me, in public, on the mouth, pushing her slippery tongue in between my lips. I close my eyes and time stops.

I spend my free time off the field playing Rubik's cube, watching MTV, or going over my card collection. At night I dream I'm Luke Skywalker fighting Darth Vader. I dream Pappy Julius is Superman in a Dodger blue uniform with a cape.

The day I had my first real kiss was the day that baseball stopped being the most important thing in my life. That's when everything changed. That day lead to everything that came after it, the string of pretty girls in high school and college, the strippers and filthy mouthed girls, the quiet church girls with the unresolved issues with their fathers, all of it. Everything gets diluted over time except the memory of that day.

Maybe this isn't about baseball after all.

That was the day that my father caught me lying, but didn't punish me. Pappy was sick and had to go to the hospital and dad couldn't find me anywhere so I never got to say goodbye like I should have. Pappy Julius was my childhood hero and at the funeral I put my Dodger's cap in the casket with him so he'd know I was always with him when they put him in the earth.

This is 1982, the year the game changed for me, forever.

39

April 1, 2008 | *BASEBALL, Fiction*

I'VE GOT DREAMS TO REMEMBER

Andrew Bomback

To the editor:

I enjoyed your baseball preview issue but wholeheartedly disagree with your predictions for the National League East. If you look at the schedules for both the Mets and the Phillies, you'll see that the Mets play twenty of their last thirty-two games at home, during which time the Phillies have eleven straight road games on the West Coast. That, in my opinion, will be the difference between who finishes first and second in what will surely be a competitive race.

In addition to predicting that my Mets will win the NL East, I have five other predictions for the upcoming season that I'd like to disclose. I leave it to your discretion as to whether you'd like to share these predictions with your readers. Feel free not to print my letter at all; alternatively, you can just stop after the first paragraph.

Samara Pearlstein

Enough of the disclaimers, though – here are five more predictions for the 2008 season.

1. I will leave work early to get to Shea Stadium in time for batting practice, and I will sit in the left field bleachers hoping to catch my first baseball in over fifteen years of going to Mets games. No balls will come my way, though, and my disappointment will linger until whichever inning the Mets first score.

2. The Mets will go another year without having a no-hitter, but early in the season, probably still in April, one of their pitchers will bring a no-hit bid into the ninth inning. With no outs or one out (but definitely not with two outs), he'll give up a clean, line-drive double down the right field line. My wife, whom I will have called into the living room during the seventh inning when the no-hitter seems like a true possibility, will pat my arm and tell me she's sorry. "No, no," I'll say, smiling. "No, it's okay. We're still going to win the game, and he pitched a hell of a game." I'll kiss her, and we'll go directly to the bedroom, before the game is over.

3. Because my wife refuses to take Memorial Day

42

weekend off, I will go alone to my ex-girlfriend's wedding. In a country club just outside of Albany, I will sneak off to the clubhouse bar and stupidly pay for drinks so that I can watch the Mets. One of the bridesmaids, still single, probably the ex-roommate of my ex-girlfriend, will find a seat next to me. She'll tell me she usually roots for the Yankees. She'll say, "I hear you're a lawyer now." "Accountant," I'll correct her. The direction this conversation takes will depend on how the Mets are doing, but, overall, nothing much will happen.

4. The Braves will sweep the Mets in a July weekend series that ends with a nationally televised Sunday night game. After the loss, I'll take a pitcher of ice water out with me to my deck along with a boom box and the two-disc Otis Redding anthology my sister bought me for Christmas this year. The Mets will be in third place after the series, and I'll consider calling in sick to work the next morning.

5. We'll still be playing in October, and we'll win the World Series, and after the last out, after the post-game interviews, after the stations switch over to non-baseball matter, I'll turn off the television. I'll put on a coat and take a walk

43

around my quiet suburban block and wish for a
few moments that I was still living in the city,
that my wife and I were ten years younger and
still had that tiny apartment in the East Village,
so that we could hear other people celebrating.
But then I'll end up back on my front lawn, which
will probably be frozen, and I'll look at my house,
and I'll stare at my dark bedroom, where my wife
will already be asleep, and I'll be happy. The Mets
will have won. And the next morning I'll tell her
all about the victory. I'll tell her that I love her.
I'll suggest maybe we should try getting pregnant
now. "Our child will be born next summer," I'll
say. "Perfect timing."

44

As the Mets once said, "Ya gotta believe!"

Sincerely,
A Believer

P.S. If you do print this letter, may I suggest as a title, "I've
Got Dreams to Remember?" It's always been my favorite
Otis Redding song.

ANDREW BOMBACK

David Kramer

April 1, 2011 | *BASEBALL, Nonfiction*

SEVENTH INNING STRETCH
Alice Lowe

America's Game: It is the place where memory gathers.
> – Walt Whitman

1.

My mother, Brooklyn-born and raised, used to tell me that if the Dodgers had been in the World Series in 1943, I might have been born at Ebbets Field. They struggled to a third-place 81-72 season, not even close to the playoffs that year, but here's the scenario as I imagine it: Game three of a subway series against the Yankees. Each team has one win, and the drama will move from Flatbush to enemy territory— the Bronx—tomorrow. "Dem Bums" need this win to keep their chances alive. My folks are in the tenth row of the right field bleachers, it's the bottom of the sixth inning, no score with two outs and two men on base. All-star second baseman and super slugger Billy Herman comes to the plate. He swings and misses. The tension is electric, and as the pitcher releases his curve ball, Lena's water breaks and she doubles over with a searing contraction. Ushers shuffle her down the steps, down the ramps, down to the bowels of the locker room, and a call comes over the PA system: "Is there a doctor in the house?" I make my entrance to the refrain of "Take Me Out to the Ballgame." My mother's first question isn't, "Is it a girl or a boy," but "Did they score?"

Katie Gross

47

2.

Is baseball still America's game, a symbol of our national grit and gumption? Football and basketball dominate televised sports and jock banter; baseball is often dismissed with one damning word: "slow." Yet for six months of the year, from early spring to the pinnacle of the playoffs, known just as "October," people of every persuasion pass through the turnstiles of the country's 30 major league ballparks. An average of 34,000-plus attend each of the 81 games that make up each team's home season; overall attendance continues to mount, barring the occasional slump, with more than 73 million attending games in 2009, a year of economic hardship. Baseball has its staunch and eloquent defenders, including *Washington Post* sportswriter Thomas Boswell, who in his 1987 "Why is Baseball So Much Better Than Football,"

succinctly sets forth the simple math: 162 games a year are 10.125 times better than 16; if you miss your NFL team's game you have to wait a week for the next one, whereas in baseball you wait a day. Baseball jargon has permeated our language—its idioms are commonplace to people who have little or no knowledge or interest in the game. Right off the bat one might hit a home run, bat a thousand, strike out, or be safe by a mile. An estimate is a ballpark figure, in the ballpark unless it's out in left field. You want to cover all the bases if you're going to score, be big league, play hardball. He's pitching woo, but she's playing the field, and he can't get to first base. I didn't make this up—I just call 'em as I see 'em.

3.

My home team is the San Diego Padres, and I'm a loyal-enough fan, but I have to confess that I'm unfaithful in my heart of hearts. My passion is for the New York Yankees—they exude irresistible charisma on the field and bring the game to life for me. They are perennial top dogs, the rottweilers of baseball, while I consider myself a champion of underdogs everywhere—the poor, the exiled, the disenfranchised. People disparage the Yanks for their vulgar riches and try to talk me around, as if I were dating someone who'd made his fortune from Ponzi schemes. I recall my father saying, tongue only partly in cheek I think, that it's just as easy to fall in love with a rich man as a poor man; someone else said that love isn't rational. I defend my ardor against all assaults. I have a couple of Yankee caps—a very smart-looking white one with navy letters, the other a mesh workout style in kind of a washed-out navy—and in my naiveté I used to tip my hat and say "go Yankees!" when I saw others sporting the nested "NY" (not to be confused with the staggered letters of the Mets). I found it curious that these were typically young guys wearing baggy low-slung pants until I learned that the rapper Jay-Z had made Yankee caps into a pop culture fashion statement. In the movie "Catch Me If You Can," the father explains his business sleight of hand to his son. The reason the Yankees win so much is the pinstripes, he says—their opponents can't take their eyes off the pinstripes. The Padres were mesmerized by the pinstripes in the 1998 World Series, outclassed, outplayed and ousted in four games, quick and painless as laser surgery. The two teams have met on the field only a few times over the years, so my loyalty is rarely challenged.

4.

Walt Whitman believed that baseball reflected the national atmosphere, as important to Americans as the

Constitution; Mark Twain saw it as the epitome of nineteenth-century America, a symbol of drive and ambition. Baseball pops up in both classic and contemporary literature, usually to invoke all things American, along with the flag, motherhood and apple pie. Novelists use a baseball milieu, players' names, or other references to describe characters, to set scenes, or to add color, to evoke that very Americanness. Yet Jane Austen wrote about it in England forty years before it was ostensibly invented in the U.S. In *Northanger Abbey*, written in 1798, Austen describes her protagonist, Catherine Morland, as having in her youth preferred "cricket, base ball, riding on horseback, and running about the country." So it would appear that baseball's American roots and birth in Cooperstown, New York in 1839 are a spurious claim, a slice of the myth created in part by Mr. Spalding of bat and glove fame. But then we didn't invent motherhood or apple pie, either. Virginia Woolf said that America has baseball in lieu of society, not as a pejorative as I first interpreted it, but rather an admission of admiration, acknowledging that we had carved through hierarchy and country houses to create our own distinctive traditions. Books written about baseball are as plentiful as fly balls to center field, regaling readers with history and lore, fish stories and anecdotes, scandals from the fixing of the 1919 World Series to current steroid and drug abuse. Sports writing can be mind-numbing and flatfooted, but in the right hands it can soar out of the park. Writers like Ring Lardner and Roger Angell portray the pathos and the poetry of the game and can bring a tear to the eye or roll-on-the-floor hoots of laughter. It was Lardner's masterpiece, *You Know Me Al,* that caught Virginia Woolf's attention and captured what for her was fresh and unique about American writing.

5.

Baseball statistics are a world unto themselves. It's said that professional baseball is the only sport where every single thing that every single player does is recorded, from heroics to pratfalls. Reciting baseball statistics can help a man postpone orgasm (so I'm told), whether because it invokes anesthetizing boredom or is such a riveting diversion that it takes his mind away from what he's doing. In addition to citings of each hitter's AB, AVG, RBI, BB, and OBP (at bats, batting average, runs batted in, bases on balls, on-base percentage), sportscasters and writers spew out numbers like lava from an erupting volcano—plate appearances, sacrifice flies, runners in scoring position, double plays and triple plays, first pitch bunts and bunts with runners on base, stolen bases, slugging average (different from batting average). And that doesn't even touch on the numbers amassed around pitching, with its quantum-physics precision and form. The records are challenges begging to be broken, memorized by kids collecting and trading baseball cards. Take home runs. There are records for numbers of home runs in a player's lifetime, in a season, a series, a game (the most is four), consecutive games (eight); by league and team; by age and handedness (right, left or switch); by field position and batting position; by whether it's inside or outside the park; by runs batted in and hitting for the cycle. It's not inconceivable to hear that someone just broke the record for the most home runs with runners in scoring position by a clean-up left-handed National League second-baseman over 35 in the month of August.

6.

Only opera outscores baseball for me as both absorbing entertainment and welcome diversion. In spite of or because of their stark differences, they complement each other, and the fact that their seasons barely overlap means that my ecstasy extends almost year-round. Several years ago, one early May, I realized the dream, an unparalleled thrill, of seeing an opera at the Met and a game at Yankee Stadium on consecutive days. My next-door neighbor's sister-in-law has attended games at every major league ballpark in the country, including new ones in New York and Minneapolis, and Japan too. Her favorite, and mine, is San Francisco's AT&T Park. Baseball with perks— the bridge, the bay, sherbet-hued sunsets, Gilroy garlic fries and crab Louie, Anchor Steam beer. San Francisco is also the second-rated vegetarian-friendly ballpark according to PETA, boasting veggie dogs and gardenburgers among the meatless treats. You'd expect no less of San Francisco, but Philadelphia ranks first, a faux chicken sandwich competing wattle to jowl with the traditional Philly Cheesesteak at Citizens Bank Park. Most ballparks have corporate sponsorship, and their names pay tribute to the largesse, a concession to economic reality. In San Diego it's Petco Park, Houston has Minute Maid, Tampa is Tropicana, many are banks. Some seem sacred—Yankee Stadium, Fenway Park, Wrigley Field—but you never know; on the South Side of Chicago, White Sox fans now go to U.S.Cellular Field instead of Comiskey Park.

7.

The seventh-inning stretch is an institution of unknown origins, and who would question it, except perhaps a child. Behind me one balmy summer San Diego evening in section 316 in the upper deck above third base, a young girl asked "Why?" Her father explained that it was tradition, a break, like halftime in football. She chewed on that, in between bites of puffy pink cotton candy, and counted on her sticky fingers before asking why again, why it wasn't halfway through the game if it was like halftime. "It just is," he said. The singing of "Take Me Out to the Ballgame" is the sacrosanct rite of the seventh-inning stretch, now often preceded, since 9/11, by "God Bless America" or followed by tokens of local color. Houston fans burst into "The Yellow Rose of Texas;" in Milwaukee they roll out the "Beer Barrel Polka." Less predictable is the Los Angeles/Anaheim Angels' "Build Me Up Buttercup" and John Denver's "Thank God I'm a Country Boy" in urban Baltimore. In his tally of baseball's advantages, Boswell compares the homespun dignity of "Take Me Out" to its flamboyant football halftime counterpart: Up With People singing "The Impossible Dream" during a Blue Angels flyover with marching bands.

8.

I played softball in P.E. classes at school. I wasn't much of an athlete, but I was whip-thin and could rocket around the bases, or catapult in pursuit of a fly ball. My first husband was a hard-throwing, left-handed pitcher (though a right-handed batter) on his college team— my mother loved that I married a baseball player. As a young officer in the Marine Corps he was exempted from more militaristic duties to hurl his fastball for the base team; he kept his pitching arm safe by managing the officers' club during the off-season. My daughter was a Bobbysoxer, an all-star batter and pitcher in minor league, but when she moved up to the majors and junior high school, there was too much competition on and off the field. After a season relegated to counting the daisies in right field and the freckles on her arms, she shifted her focus to boys and clothes. My grandson played Little League, starting at five with T-ball—tiny tykes swinging eagerly, determinedly, sometimes tearfully, in a fierce contest with a stationary ball—to the finely honed and competitively groomed majors. I cheered him from the stands, sporting the caps and colors of his teams—Padres, Cardinals, Rockies. Cory didn't pursue baseball when he got to high school, but it continued to be a bond between us that included our shared allegiance to the Yankees. He believed that his grandma knew more about baseball than just about anyone, certainly more than any female. We would hash it all out, players and playoff chances, trades and gossip and stats; I had to stay on top of my game to secure my image and that of all womanhood in his eyes.

9.

We lived in New York until I was six. Nowadays parents lug infants in carriers to games, but small children were more likely left at home back then. I was foisted onto neighbors when my parents would take my brother, five years older, to games at Ebbets Field, Yankee Stadium and the Polo Grounds, wearing his Babe Ruth number-three pinstripe uniform. "No fair!" I scowl on behalf of my innocent and ignorant small self as David recalls clear memories from those distant and to me indistinct days. Mom gladly exchanged the northeast's extremes of winter and summer for California's placid sameness, but she left something intangible behind—that part of her spirit that was tethered to her roots and everything she'd known. To baseball, which she continued to follow on radio and then television, a scorecard and her knitting on her lap, alternating pencil and needles. When her beloved Bums followed us west some years later, she welcomed them like prodigal sons. We didn't have the ways or means to make more than a few road trips from San Diego to Los Angeles over the years, but they were sacred occasions for her. She always kept a scorecard to track, with painstaking accuracy, the hieroglyphics that translated into every play of the game. As a teenager I didn't like the long drives with my parents; I was bored by the game and would occupy myself by picking out cute players with the binoculars. My most vivid recollection of Dodger Stadium is the discovery of Gulden's tangy ochre-brown mustard—who knew there was an alternative to French's screaming yellow? Perhaps those trips planted the seeds of an animosity toward the Dodgers that I cultivate to this day. Then it was the need to forge my own distinctive identity; now it's the Dodgers' display of Hollywood hubris and the fact that they're arch-enemies of the Padres (and formerly of the Yankees). Or maybe it's just my own tradition. I like to think that my mother, always a New Yorker, would have accepted my proclivities with a shrug and said, "waddaya gonna do?"

April 1, 2012 | *BASEBALL, Nonfiction*

THE DAY THE MUSIC SHOULD HAVE DIED: GAME 7 OF THE 1979 WORLD SERIES

Ben Lyon

We are family
I got all my sisters with me

Do you know the song "We are Family" by Sister Sledge? Of course you do; you don't even need to think about it. When you were nine, in your early self-exploration of pop music, when everything was new, did you think it was pretty amazing? When you were a teenager, was listening to it as shameful as masturbating in your parent's basement? Have you listened to it all the way through in your adult life? Does hearing it even for a second on some FM station today make you kinda sad for everybody, and force you to gaze off into the distance? Turns out, it gets worse: "We are Family" is no mere Best of the 70's, 80's and 90's touchstone; in 1979, it served as the anthem for the World Series winner, the Pittsburg Pirates. It's so intertwined with that team it's mentioned in the first paragraph of their Wikipedia entry.

Speaking of oft visited Wikipedia entries, would Paul Bunyan have liked sports? How much better would American history be if Paul Bunyan actually lived? Should we all just pretend he did? Would you find

57

Nick Francis Potter

secret joy in Paul Bunyan beating the holy hell out of Johnny Appleseed? Well, there was a Paul Bunyan-esque sports fan once: Wild Bill Hagy. He drove a cab, had long hair and a longer beard, wore a cowboy hat, jorts and striped socks and was the "cheerleader" for the 1979 World Series loser, the Baltimore Orioles. Wild Bill would lead the upper deck of Memorial Stadium in an O-R-I-O-L-E-S cheer (amongst others) almost every night. Was Paul Bunyan a heavy drinker? Well, as there probably wasn't much else to do in Minnesota in the 1800's, all signs point toward "Of fucking course he was," but even a drunken Paul Bunyan couldn't compare to Wild Bill—who, in pure Bunyan style, brought his own beer to every game he attended. And when he was barred from doing this, he stopped going to games. That's the dedication Wild Bill had to the Orioles—he knew they'd want him at his best, and his best meant plowed.

But that song. That song! Even before the 1979 series, if you played "We are Family" in front of Wild Bill or his friends—and they were all his friends—you could most likely expect a broken bottle to come raining down upon your dome.

And our goal's in sight
We know we don't get depressed

My father, Fred, and uncle, nicknamed Ace, were O's fans back then, and along with Wild Bill, followed them as they went 102-57, won the pennant, and headed to the World Series. The O's got off to an excellent start in the 1979 Series, taking a 3-games-to-1 lead. They lost games five and six, setting up a deciding game seven to be played at the O's Memorial Stadium. In 1979, you could buy tickets to Game Seven of the World Series even if you weren't a Koch brother, and Fred and Ace did just that, mounting a rambling burp of a bus to make the 90 minute trip.

It was a brave act. The O's were poised to achieve the rare double indignity of blowing a 3-1 series lead and losing the final two games at home.

The O's did achieve the double indignity. Like stunned, well-meaning frat boys, they crapped the bed in games five, six, and seven. Lost them by a cumulative score of 15-3. Worse, maybe, was that none of these games were instant classics; they were the type of games that get played every day during the baseball season. The O's did manage to give up two runs in the top of the ninth in game seven, turning a tight 2-1 thriller into a 4-1 inevitability, but no single moment defines this series. That mantle was, instead, taken up by the disco stylings of the Sledge. Loving life is fun!

The lack of fight in the O's particularly infuriated my dad and his brother. They felt it in their very marrow, they felt it in their sinuses. The bland death the Orioles laid down to accept created a backwave of fury that whomped into the stands, crashing down on the seats holding two disgusted brothers. Here was the fury Fred and Ace and Wild Bill and all the rest of them wanted to see blasting out of the O's! Why hadn't they gotten mad? Why?

Fred and Ace got mad. Enough for the O's, enough for everyone. Fred and Ace threw down. They looked around, picked the inevitable fight with Pirates fans. Aw, shaddup, they were told. Not even a punch thrown. Their mouths ached with the absence of slug. The opposite of sated. They did what any self-respecting family member did: they got on the bus, and they fought each other.

Fred: Jesus that was a train wreck
Ace: Yep

Fred: What a choke

Ace: Yep

Fred: Les Boulez[1] should be good though

Ace: Yeah

Fred: I swear to Christ Al Bumbry is fucking awful

Ace: Wait what?

Fred: You realize that Al Bumbry just went 3 for 21 in the G.D. World Series RIGHT?

Ace: You realize that Al Bumbry hit .285 while playing a very solid centerfield right all year right?

Fred: HOLY SHIT YOU HAVE NEVER BEEN MORE WRONG ABOUT ANYTHING IN YOUR LIFE

I'm figuring it's hard to yell at somebody on a bus. Sitting side by side, you'd have to contort your body so it's up against some cheap plastic armrest to really get in a good position. But if you're committed, you don't let the particular ergonomics of a bus stop you. Fred and Ace were unstoppable, it could be said.

In the Pirates locker room, deep man hugs were exchanged, champagne was guzzled, "We are Family" was pumped from the speakers. Legacies were cemented. On a bus chugging toward D.C., Fred and Ace were getting operatic about Al Bumbry. A different kind of legacy. It was the start of the end for Wild Bill's baseball. I don't know what Wild Bill Hagy did the night after

---

1. Point of order: Les Boulez wasn't used to discuss the Bullets until Tony Kornheiser created it in the late 1980's. So that phrase wouldn't have been uttered on the bus. However, the laws of decency now require all reference to the Bullets to be made by calling them Les Boulez — anybody who says "Bullets" wasn't there. They didn't live it. They have no idea who Mitchell Butler was or could have been.

BENJAMIN LYON

Game Seven ended, but my father and his brother were conducting the funeral rites for him. In the only way possible: loudly and angrily.

Living life is fun and we've just begun
To get our share of the world's delights

> Fred: OK, WE'RE FUCKING DONE HERE
> Ace: NO SHIT
> Fred: I'll talk to you at Christmas...1980

Can we admit baseball has gotten a little twee? George Will, Ken Burns, Field of Dreams, NPR-approved indie rock as the soundtrack. Wild Bill Hagy wouldn't have given a shit about any of that. The baseball cognoscenti feels obliged to compare any exciting moment with the American experience. Look, the last game of the 2011 regular season was amazing (in part because the High Lords of twee, the Red Sox, collapsed in flaming ruin) but did we need to get all weepy-eyed? Did SportsCenter anchors have to lecture us on how much we should appreciate it? Did the corpse of Robert Frost have to be dragged out and forced to write a poem celebrating the chock of a hit, the perfect American base? Is that the part of the game Wild Bill loved? W.W.W.B.H.D., everybody!

Would Wild Bill ever say, "Wow, this game sure is romantic, and such a metaphor for life! Someone hand me a pencil!" Sure, he might say that, but he'd be slowly pouring a beer onto your Keds as he did.

It's time to reverse course. We need to bring our own beer into stadiums—jammed in to the pockets of the parka you're wearing in July, or disguised in Coke bottles, or blatantly carried in because, remember, W.W.W.B.H.D.—we need to make up chants for about every batter—and the opposing team's pitcher's sister—we need to wear jean shorts. And then we need to go home and never try to tie what we just saw back to the industrial revolution.

And we're good on family. No more "We Are Family"; a two-year moratorium on father and sons playing catch. Wild Bill didn't need to tie the game into a familial experience and my father and brother riding on that bus didn't feel closer to each other; they hated each other. And that was real. You get pissed and drunk and angry after something like that Game Seven. You say awful things but those awful things are you. They're authentic and of the moment. More authentic than Kevin Costner walking slowly toward Ray Liotta.

It's still a great game—still pretty much the same game Wild Bill Hagy loved in 1979. The game doesn't need to be overhauled to be great again, just stripped down, made more sleek and new and forward looking. Nothing too drastic; I'm not talking about turning it into some sports car. More like turning it into Wild Bill Hagy's cab. Because, though it didn't look like much, that cab could move man, it could really move.

April 1, 2012 | *BASEBALL, Nonfiction*

Baseball is Poetry
Sam Anderson-Ramos

Mike Hampton - P

When I wore my Astros hat and jersey to see them play the Cubs at Wrigley Field, someone threw a tampon at me, still in its wrapper. I didn't see who threw it.

Tony Eusebio – C

After another Astros-Cubs game at Wrigley, as I made my way through the crowd, a guy, about my age, shouted, "Fuck the Astros!" in my face, then disappeared.

Jeff Bagwell - 1B

I grew up in Austin, Texas. My dad used to drive me to Houston to see the Astros play. The Astrodome was a vast, ugly place for baseball. It had all the coziness of a window fan. The green Astroturf was stained in a way real grass never could be. The rainbow-colored upper levels were always empty, except for one or two random fans, their heads back, asleep.

Craig Biggio - 2B

I knew much more about baseball than my dad did. When we went to games I told him who the players were. I taught myself how to keep score.

My dad umpired one of my

little league games once. He bought a clicker to keep track of the outs. Several times he called a strike a ball, even when the batter swung and missed. When he called a foul ball fair one of the kids on the other team asked me what I thought. I admitted the umpire got the call wrong. I felt like a bad son, but it was true. My dad got the call very wrong.

After the game our coach faced the stands and loudly scolded the crowd for booing my dad. She said Mr. Ramos had been the only one with the guts to volunteer.

Ken Caminiti - 3B

In fifth grade I played catch with my best friend, Chris. One day Chris threw the ball as high as he could. I lost it in the sun and the ball smashed my face. When my dad saw my busted lip he was mad at Chris, but I knew it was my fault. I should've made the catch.

Ricky Gutierrez - SS

I had a bully. When my bully challenged me to strike him out I was prepared. I used to practice pitching in our backyard, only fastballs because I didn't know how to throw anything else.

I threw two pitches. The first was right down the middle. It clipped the strike zone I'd marked on an abandoned piece of plywood. My bully watched it go by.

"Strike one," Chris called from the sidelines.

"Ooh," my bully said, eyes wide.

The next pitch was just as good, but this time my bully swung and connected. The ball flew about four backyards away. I don't remember if my bully rounded the bases. The bases weren't really bases anyway. They were trees, except first base. That was the porch.

Aaron Alford

Matt Mieske – LF

I used to go to my backyard when it was dark and hit baseballs from the porch into the trees beyond our fence. I'd toss the ball in the air and hit it on the way down. The good ones flew over the telephone wires above the tree line.

When I didn't have a ball I used rocks that left scars in my wood bats.

Carl Everett – CF

The only game my mom ever took me to was a playoff game at the Astrodome. There were over 54, 000 people in attendance, the largest crowd in Dome history. My mom cheered as if she knew what was going on. I shared a high-five with a stranger three times my age. The Astros were ahead, and then they weren't, and then the game was over. My heart was broken.

Afterward my mom drove us back to Austin. It was late by then, and we wouldn't be home until after midnight. My SAT's were the next morning. I took a practice test in my prep book during the drive.

Derek Bell – RF

The only time I ever heard a tornado siren was at Wrigley Field. It was a night game, and the Astros were in town. It was one of the first games my girlfriend, Sarah, and I ever went to together. She grew up in Winnetka. Her dad raised her on the Cubs.

There was some rain and the game was delayed. When the rain let up the game resumed. A couple of innings later there was thunder and some distant flashes in the clouds, but the game went on.

There was no rain in the air when a bolt of lightning struck about four blocks away. Lance Berkman,

SAM ANDERSON-RAMOS

the Astros first baseman, jumped several inches off the ground, ducked his head, then ran off the field. The umpire waved his arms. The rain came down.

Sarah and I decided to wait and see if the rain would stop and the game would continue. I left for ice cream. The crowd under the stands was boisterous but orderly. I bought one hotdog and two chocolate scoops in styrofoam cups. I put the hotdog in my pocket and held one chocolate scoop in each hand.

I was nearing the passageway to the field when the siren began. It sounded like an air-raid warning, a long wail that slowly rose and lowered in pitch. I looked past the yellow-jacketed usher in the passageway to where the field was supposed to be, but all I could see was a glowing swirl of horizontal rain. I was convinced the tornado had entered the stadium, and that Sarah was in mortal danger. I had never felt so confronted by a natural force, so moved by its power. I was terrified. The usher stared into space. I didn't understand how she could be so calm. I considered abandoning the ice cream. Instead I took a breath, passed the usher, and entered the passageway, not sure what I would find when I emerged.

I was relieved to learn that the rain and wind weren't as tumultuous as they'd seemed. The field was still there, and the city, steamed by the mid-summer storm.

Then I saw Sarah, a few aisles above where our seats had been, under an awning with two hundred rowdy super fans, plastic beer cups in hand. She was standing. When she caught my eye she waved, and I brought the ice cream to her.

April 16, 2013 | *BASEBALL, Fiction*

THE UMPIRE
Eric Nusbaum

The thought of home was more than he could bear. The sunk-in feeling of his recliner, the smell of Linda's pot roast, the weight of her body pressed up against his in the bedroom doorway -- all of it was just too much. The umpire deserved no such comforts. He deserved exactly what he had, exactly this: to fumble with tiny bottles from the mini-bar, to stare into the depths of the pale, floral wallpaper, to channel surf, carefully skipping the local news, the cable news, and especially the sports networks. Sitcoms were safe, pre-recorded late-night talk shows, *Law and Order*, old movies, pay-per-view.

After the game, the umpire shook the kid's hand and apologized. The press room was too bright, microphones stuck under his nose like a bouquet of plastic flowers. But he could hardly talk. All he could do was remember the kid's eyes, all glassy and damaged like a pair of jellyfish drying up on the beach. The umpire was sure he would always remember those eyes.

Nick Francis Potter

Later, safely ensconced in the hotel room, he said "Linda. Linda. Linda. What happened?"

"You're a human being," Linda said.

"That's the problem."

He laughed. She laughed. He hung up the phone.

It was a groundball. Nothing less, nothing more. The umpire could see the pitch perfectly: a sinker low and inside, driving down toward the batter's ankles. He could see the swing, a half-assed check swing was all it was, and hear the click of the ball against the bat. Nothing more than a click. Then the ball tumbling forward over the grass toward second base.

The hotel room had two beds in it, but neither was working. This was Detroit, so the room was decorated with pictures from the glory years of American manufacturing. Above one of the beds hung a stylized photo of the factory floor of a Ford plant in the 1950s. The workers were tiny and purposeful, all in motion. Peak efficiency. The umpire's father had been a machinist in a factory that made airplane parts, and had told him to always focus. If you don't focus you could lose a finger. I've seen it happen.

Some jobs are inherently futile, the umpire thought. He was pacing and eating potato chips from a plastic tube.

70

The clock radio said 3:17 and was playing some kind of symphony. Classical musicians are supposed to reproduce great works flawlessly, practically erasing themselves in the process. It seemed impossible. Umpiring was impossible, too. You had to be invisible but also everywhere at once. The umpire had blown calls before. This was different. Normally, it was a case of obstructed vision; a case of too close to call, tie goes to the runner (a real rule because there had to be a rule).

Topspin. He remembered topspin, and he remembered the batter charging up the first base line toward him, plowing golden dirt with his cleats. He remembered the throw to first, the runner's foot crashing against the bag. Too late. Too late, he could remember saying to himself. But which was too late? The runner or the throw? The throw or the runner? A series of flashes went off behind his eyes, like somebody was taking pictures inside his skull.

He was in the bathroom now, staring at himself in the mirror. The umpire's hair was gray and his gut hung over his belt, but otherwise not so bad. He was a solid man, solidness having always been important to him. It was the inherent belief in his solidness that led him to umpiring school after he finished college in Toledo, Ohio. He would be a high school history teacher from September to June and umpire during the summer. Nothing would be absent

71

from his life. At least that was the idea. The umpire had always trusted completely in his own impartiality, which he now realized was absurd. He walked over to the light-switch and flipped it on and off for a few moments, thinking perhaps he could recreate the flashes. But nothing happened. He turned on the shower.

In the shower the umpire thought about human error. He had committed a human error. It was the same thing they said about plane crashes and nuclear meltdowns. He liked the phrase because if you thought about it a certain way, his mistake could be ascribed to something bigger; the entire sequence could be evolution's fault. Human error, like moose error, like salmon error, like dog error. Not umpire error. In this context it was not so bad. He was not so bad. This would all be swallowed up by time anyway. The umpire turned off the shower, and the room was very quiet.

He remembered the stadium's quiet. The collective, anticipatory inhale of thirty thousand fans. It was so quiet the umpire could hear the sweaty first base coach scratching his ass a few feet away. He remembered the flashes disappearing from behind his eyes, his arms being raised by some force, some subconscious anti-gravitational force, and the word SAFE coming out of his mouth. The thirty thousand fans still silent. The kid on

ERIC NUSBAUM,

the mound silent, too. The word SAFE echoing upward into the night.

The umpire opened a curtain and exposed the shadows of the cityscape. The sky was beginning to turn from black to blue. Soon enough he would have to go outside and face Detroit, face all of it. Looking out on the tops of buildings, he realized that there was some poetry to all of this, baseball being a sport predicated on failure, a sport in which perfection of any kind is rare. The only person expected to be perfect on a baseball field is the umpire.

73

Killian Czuba

April 17, 2013 | *BASEBALL, Fiction*

THE LONELINESS OF THE DESIGNATED PINCH RUNNER

Terrance Wedin

Sunday, October 13th, 1974
Dodger Stadium, Los Angeles, CA

In the dugout, waiting to run.

The whole game memorizing the pale swirls in the concrete floor of the Dodgers's visiting dugout. Down three, the swirls have Wash making strange associations: creamed coffee, his wife's shoulder, a painting of birds he remembers from grade school. Wash watches the sun set from the bench, the burn of the stadium lights coming to life. The slowness of the sport has never appealed to him. He can only stand the calm for so long.

End of the eighth, Coach Irv jogs in from the third base box. Light jumps around his green Athletics jacket.

Irv's hand moves from his pouch of Red Man to his bottom lip.

"Legs good?" Irv asks.

"Ready to book," Wash says.

"We get on, you might go."

"Good," Wash says. "I've been waiting for something to happen."

"Need to go over the signs?"

"I got the signs."

"Don't miss your blessings," Irv says, spitting into the swirls. "Hard to come in cold, I know."

"Can't steal second with a foot on first," Wash says.

The drive from the hotel to the stadium that morning: the asphalt, the heat, the traffic. His wife getting up from the bed to wash her face. The way she kissed his chin before he left. Keeping his head in the season has been tough. The travel days wear him down. He loses track of his teammates names, innings, the score. When he does get to run, it's never for long enough. The coaches tease him: let him take BP, shag fly balls with the outfielders. But his swing is too slow, his arm too weak, his glove lazy. He's a runner, not a baseball player. He was hired for his legs.

Top of the ninth, the Dodgers fall apart. Sutton beans Brando, Reggie knocks a liner to the corner, and Rudi drives them both home. The stadium bends into a roar. It's a sound Wash could lose track of the world inside, wrap around himself like a blanket, sleep. It's the same feeling that hit him at track meets, way back.

Alvin, the skip, calls from across the dugout, waking Wash from his daydream.

"You're a go," Alvin says.

Wash feels electric, full of meaning, his white cleats clicking up the concrete stairs, leaving his head and those dirty swirls back in the dugout. He watches Marshall take his warm-ups on the mound. He tries spying a tell in his delivery. He shakes out his legs like he's done since his freshman year of high school track. He high steps, and the polyester of his uniform sticks to his skin. He has never belonged on this team. Every time he was picked off during the regular season, he jogged back to the dugout staring at the bat rack, instead of meeting his teammates eyes. If he can't run, then what? Then he is Finley's failed experiment. He misses running track. If he lost a race or got poor start off the blocks it was all on him. He could punish his body with circuit sprints until he puked. He could work through the mistakes on his own. Being in baseball meant his mistakes were owned by thousands and thousands of people.

His name reverberates through the PA system.

The bag is World Series soft under his heel, pillowy even. Off it, he stabs his toes into the springy dirt in front of first. He dangles his arm between his stance. He twitches his fingers like he's playing an imaginary

77

trumpet, an attempt at distraction. Garvey, the first basemen leans in, angles his body so his big glove points at Marshall, who shakes down signs from home. Wash side steps, getting that much closer to being gone.

Irv signs at Wash from the box: touches his head, swipes the yellow and green logo on his chest, touches his left wrist. All of this means something. The bodies in the crowd behind Irv swirl into Wash's vision. This means something, too.

On the mound, Marshall sets his body still. He rests his tanned glove against his chest. He waits.

Wash takes another side step, a little one. The dirt, the stadium lights, the dark navy sky beyond the lights, the city beyond the stadium. Wash is connected to none of it out there, off the bag. Off far enough that he can't dive back. Out where nobody can help him: not Irv giving him signs, not Alvin in the dugout, not Fosse at the plate, not his wife in the crowd, watching with the other player's wives. It feels familiar, that loneliness.

He dives back, anyway. Because what else can he do?

Garvey's glove, fat with the ball now, stings his hand hard. Garvey's breathing is heavy and rhythmic and hot on Wash's cheek. It's intimate, how close they are. The ump, another body, breaks the moment, fist clutched in the air. Out.

Wash brushes off his uniform. The crowd cheers and boos as he jogs back to the dugout. It's a crushing, damaged sound. The scoreboard leaks into his vision, the deficit blurs. There is more life beyond this moment, he knows. It's painful, though, this moment. The faces of his teammates and coaches in the dugout swirl. They look washed out, all the same now, nameless. He takes his seat on the bench. Alone, again. An errant trashcan lid, pancakes, the clouds in Mississippi. He waits for the final out so he can shower up and take the freeway back to the hotel.

79

April 22, 2013 | *BASEBALL, Nonfiction*

PREDICTIONS

T.S. Flynn

We made it. The 2013 Major League Baseball season is right there in front of us, a vast expanse of fastballs and line drives, diving stops and crisp throws, attaboys and errors, beers and hot dogs. The postseason is still just a smudge on the horizon, blurred beyond recognition by the quivering heat of July and August. And you expect me to accurately predict the fates of thirty teams assembled by committee? Okay, sure. But let's not get ahead of ourselves. I didn't fall in love with baseball for the short-burst glory of the postseason. It's the months of unpredictability before the playoffs that hooked me.

Baseball is about homestands and road trips packed with unpredictable moments. Some of them are even unforgettable. When I think about the moments that have lingered for the nearly forty years I've been a fan, very few have anything to do with how my White Sox finished. Winning it all in 2005 isn't something I'd ever give back, but seeing the final out of that World Series was special because of all the small moments that preceded it that season and the other thirty seasons I'd been a fan. For instance, those moments back in 1990, when a friend and I took our sweet time leaving old Comiskey Park after the final out of the last game I'd ever see there, my first as an adult. An usher spotted us lingering at the rail above the box seats. He waved, encouraging us to walk down to the seats behind

Samara Pearlstein

home plate. He knew this was where I'd been introduced to big league ball, where I'd become a fan. He must have. "Have a seat," he said. "There's time."

Those front row seats were about three sections and five years removed from another unpredictable moment at that great old ballpark. Returning from the concourse to the seats Grandpa had bought for us, I froze when a foul ball humpbacked in my direction. I didn't know what to do. Drop the Coke? Make a one-handed grab? Duck? In that instant of indecision a man bumped me out of the way and made the catch.

I don't remember my first-ever Comiskey Park visit, but I remember my first trip to Wrigley Field. I was seven. For most of the ninety-minute drive to Chicago Uncle Joe stressed the magnitude of the event. "You're gonna see the best pitcher in the majors today," he told the carload of cousins and neighbor kids. "Tom

Seaver. Tom Terrific." To be honest, I don't remember much about the game that afternoon. But I remember it was hot and sticky humid, and I remember that I didn't want to take my eyes off the field because Tom Sever, the best pitcher in the majors, was right there. Who could've predicted my bladder would give way before the 7th Inning Stretch? I sat for an inning, miserable in sopping Toughskins jeans before I told Uncle Joe what had happened.

Most of my memories are better than that, but each was unpredictable. Like that Sunday afternoon game at Coors Field in '96. I was with a date. We'd arrived late to our seats in the front row in center field, when the crack of the bat snapped my attention from the beer I'd slipped into the cup holder. Shouts rose and fans climbed over nearby seats. I scanned the space above the field and spotted the ball, a high line-drive heading straight for

T.S. FLYNN

us. This time I was ready. I cupped my hands on top of the padded wall. The ball began its slight descent. It would be close, but I didn't want to interfere, so I kept my hands still, calculating the geometry and physics of the approaching ball as best I could. Holy shit! It's mine! Then I heard Lenny Dykstra's spikes digging in the warning track, sh-thck, sh-thck. Then Lenny Dykstra's glove was there—right there! And then the ball found his mitt, fff-thwap, and Lenny Dykstra crashed into the wall and I swear to God I heard him grunt and goosebumps rose on my arms and my neck and I couldn't stop giggling the rest of the afternoon.

It didn't matter that I was pulling for the Rockies that day, that a visiting player gave me such a thrill. That's baseball. Watch long enough and the moments pile up. Unpredictable moments like seeing Eric Young homer on the very first pitch of the very first Rockies home game in 1993. Just seconds before he swung I would've sworn that nothing could make me happier than simply sitting at a Major League game in my hometown. For the first decades of my life, Major League Baseball had been something I saw only on vacation. I grew up with AAA ball in Denver. On a good day the Bears played for 15,000 fans and more than 50,000 empty seats. But on July 4, 1979 I was one of 60,000 fans who came out for fireworks and saw Tim Raines sprint around the bases for a 10th-inning, game-winning inside the park home run.

I thought about that magic night when I sat in the same upper deck of Mile High Stadium seventeen years later and watched young Barry Bonds leg out a triple. And I thought about that triple when my brother and I sat in the upper deck at Yankee Stadium and watched a not-so-young Barry Bonds crush his first home run at The House that Ruth Built.

I can't think about Yankee Stadium without thinking about my first visit to Fenway Park in 1999, a side trip while vacationing with the woman who would become my wife. It was The Summer of Pedro Martinez, and he was scheduled to start against the Mariners. Fans waved Dominican flags and the sold-out ballpark filled quickly. The air buzzed. I knew we had good seats, Row C, but it wasn't until the usher pointed them out that I realized we'd be sitting in the first row behind the Mariners dugout. That was just the first surprise of the afternoon.

Soon the fans near us passed along what someone had heard on the radio: Pedro had been scratched for arriving late. We still saw him pitch that day, though; he worked four innings in relief and picked up the win in the final regular season relief appearance of his career. All the Pedro drama aside, it's still one of the most memorable games I've attended. I made eye contact with Ken Griffey Jr., I saw a monster Alex Rodriguez home run to center and, best of all, we had front-row seats for a Lou Piniella ejection.

The moments pile up when

84

T. S. Flynn

you watch. I couldn't have predicted that Orlando Cabrera would outperform Vladimir Guerrero when I saw the Expos beat the Mets in Montreal during our honeymoon in September 2000. Or that, while visiting Chicago to celebrate our fifth anniversary, Mrs. Flynn and I would see Vlad's Angels beat the Sox when he scored from first on a bunt in the 12th inning. Or that I'd end up living in Minneapolis and see Jim Thome beat my team, his former team, in 2010 with the first-ever walk-off home run at Target Field.

Watch baseball and the memories pile up, or they drift away, because memory is the most unpredictable part of it all. But I'm settling into the habits of a guy in his forties now, and I can predict with certainty that I will spend most of Opening Week on a couch while dozens of streamed games wash over me like the healing waters of Lourdes. Soon after, the regenerative power of the first week of ballgames will break the inertia of the winter and I will feel compelled to see the local nine in person—never mind that they are the rebuilding Twins and my team's divisional rival. I'll go, again and again, because it's big league ball, and because you just never know what's going to happen.

Katie Gross

April 26, 2013 | *BASEBALL, Fiction*

HANDS OF GRACE

James Yates

September 13, 1998

Murphy's was packed beyond any regard to occupancy regulations, and this made Evan both grateful and concerned. With so many people around him, it was physically impossible to stumble or fall down. But this made it hard to spot his man. He tried to scan the patrons and keep an eye on the entrance as well. Yes, there would be other chances. But the magic of the afternoon had morphed into an all-encompassing delirium. All Evan wanted was to meet him. He didn't know what he would say or do, but at the very least, good eye contact and a firm handshake would suffice. Definitely the handshake.

* * *

Earlier in the afternoon, Evan shook another Winston out of his pack, unable to take his eyes off the television.

A magazine article mentioned Mark Grace's penchant for the brand, and Evan made the switch despite the noxious smoke that tasted like an industrial smokestack in Gary, Indiana. The crowds inside and outside Wrigley with almost equal numbers cheered and yelled, but he was transfixed for different reasons. It was the bottom of the ninth. Grace was in the batter's box, glaring, looking so damn All-American with that crew cut and eye black, gripping his bat, taking a few practice swings as Eric Plunk got into his windup. Evan opened an Old Style with its quiet "pssst," like the can was going to let him in on a secret. The crowds were frantic after hours in the Indian summer heat, the home run record, the back-and-forth between the Cubs and the Brewers. They all wanted to see Sammy Sosa. Evan had Grace all to himself.

Megan's keys jingled outside the door, and he sat up straight in his armchair. She walked in and made her choreographed Sunday movements, dropping her bag on the side table and taking a left turn into the kitchen. Evan heard ice cubes tinkling into the glass. She came into the living room and eased onto the loveseat, sipping her Jameson.

"Fuck. What a day."

"Hm, long one?" Evan returned his focus on Grace. The 1-1.

"I, just, how many times do I have to tell Mike to make sure my register is ready—"

James Yates

"Fuck." Evan grumbled as Grace swung and made good contact, but hit a harmless ground ball to second base.

"—before I clock in. I mean, it wasn't that busy. Everyone's watching this game, but still."

Sosa was up and everyone went apeshit. In the fifth inning, he hit his sixty-first home run of the season, a two-run shot out onto Waveland. Of course nobody would remember the two-run part. Grace had singled to right field before Sosa batted. The announcers kept going on about Sosa's RBI total. Hell, if Grace hit in front of him more often—

"Sorry, I guess you're busy." She took another long sip.

"Well, you should talk to him about it."

"I have. Many, many times. How many times have I complained to *you* about it?"

"Well, Christ *I* can't do anything about it."

"*The 2-1. Swung on, belted, there it goes! Number 62! Move over, Big Mac, you've got company!*"

Sosa ran around the bases and into the dugout. The fans screamed and threw bottles and wrappers into the outfield, that American form of celebration. Play-by-play announcer Chip Caray went off on some ramble about history and emotions, momentarily distracted from his non-stop blathering about the day's Beanie Baby giveaway, while Sosa took two curtain calls and waved.

89

"He did it!" Megan clapped. She was the most casual of casual baseball fans, but everyone in the city was at least aware of the history being made.

Evan rolled his eyes. "Yeah, they just like the spectacle and home runs. They don't care about—"

Megan finished his sentence. "—the ins and outs of the game. The way Grace plays." She stared at him for several seconds. He waited. Nothing. She turned back to the television.

He always touted Grace's underrated prowess to anyone who would listen. Grace just *looked* like a ballplayer. There was his glare, but then his warm smiles. The tanned, blonde-haired forearms and no batting gloves. Evan wanted to shake and inspect the hands. They were probably sandpapery and callused. Working man hands, those hands of Grace. In the bottom of the third, he had slid hard into second base for a double and got his helmet knocked off. That was true effort, more than Sosa running into the outfield and doing his nonsensical heart and mouth tap.

The Cubs tied the game on Gary Gaetti's single up the middle. There was a chance Sosa would get another at-bat, a chance to surpass Mark McGwire. Evan finished his beer and opened another. In the top of the tenth inning, Greg Martinez hit a grounder to first. Grace grabbed it, lunged, and applied the out tag at the last second. Evan gasped. "Oh god."

Megan finished her drink in silence.

In the bottom of the tenth, Lance Johnson grounded out to second. Jose Hernandez lined out to right field. Grace was up again, but of course nobody cared. Sosa was on deck. Al Reyes went into his windup.

Megan turned. "After the game, I was thinking—"

Evan collapsed to his knees, screaming as Grace hit the first pitch deep to right field. Walk-off home run. Cubs 11, Brewers 10.

"You son of a bitch! You did it!" Evan staggered as he got up, toasting the television. "See? What have I told you? He's the best. Nobody gives two fucking shits about Grace. Now look. Look at him!"

Megan stood up. "As I was going to say, after the game I was thinking you could head down to the ballpark and suck him off." She walked into the bedroom and slammed the door.

91

* * *

Evan left the apartment, managed to hail a cab, and got out in a tangled mesh of sweaty, sunburned fans. It took twice as long to get into the bar. He somehow got in past the bouncer, who was overwhelmed and outnumbered. Evan squeezed in, screamed "Old Style" over the din, and kept watch. Every handsome blonde crew cut was a false alarm. But he waited for Grace. And waited. Even if he never showed up, Evan would meet him in the future. It had to happen. He'd walk over confidently, slap Grace on the back, insist on buying him a drink, and tell the man how he kept vigil. How he wanted him to show up at Murphy's, but knew he was probably getting mobbed and beer-showered in the clubhouse. As late afternoon turned into early evening, he found an empty stool and ordered another Old Style. He turned to face the entrance and waited some more.

92

A PHAN'S NOTES:
THE PROFESSIONAL BALLPLAYER

Justin St. Germain

As I write this, on a Friday afternoon in early August, the Phillies are losing 7-2 in Washington, and Scott Hairston is walking up to the plate to pinch-hit for the Nationals. My phone is vibrating continually, because my book comes out in four days, but I won't discuss that at any length here; the asshole potential in discussing my own book's release seems astronomical, and besides, I want to talk about Scott Hairston.

His current at-bat comes late in a lost season for two teams currently embroiled in a tepid race for second. Their playoff hopes exist only in the most theoretical sense, and the sparse and tranquil crowd at Nationals Park reflects the situation. Even if this game did matter, the Nats are up six with one inning left to play, and the woeful Philly offense rarely scores six runs in a game, much less an inning. This is about as meaningless as an at-bat gets.

Not that you could tell from Hairston's approach. He settles into his placid stance, the barrel of the bat high and nearly vertical, tracing tiny circles like a flagpole in a swirling wind. He takes the first pitch, a meaty fastball over the heart of the plate, as well as the next three, another fastball and two sliders. It's 2-2 before his bat even moves. He lunges at the next offering, protecting the plate, but yanks it foul down the third-base line, and stares at his bat as he steps back into the box, scolding himself for trying to pull an outside fastball. The next pitch is up and in; he hits it foul in almost exactly the same spot. Only then, seven pitches into the at-bat, does he get the one he's been waiting for, a Frisbee slider that he reaches down and smashes into left-center. It carries over the fielder's head and hits the base of the wall, and Hairston hustles into second with a textbook pop-up slide, no clapping or pointing to the sky or any of the common celebration rituals, not so much as a smile as he reaches down to adjust his socks. Although his hit came at the expense of my Phillies, I clap at the TV. I don't cheer just because it was a great at-bat. Despite his former Metdom, and despite his historical abuse of my favorite team, I don't dislike Scott Hairston. In fact, he's one of my favorite players. He was the first major leaguer I ever met.

In the fall of 1999, Scott and I were classmates in an Intro to Philosophy course at a junior college in Coolidge, Arizona, a town whose name is something of a misnomer: it was 115 degrees the day we moved into the dorms. Scott was there because the baseball team was among the best in the country (he played alongside two other major leaguers, Rich Harden and Ian Kinsler). I was there because I lacked any better options for higher education, and because I still clung to some asinine plan of playing a college sport, despite a few glaring preclusions: I wasn't a great high school athlete, had spent my whole postgraduate summer chain-smoking and eating Whoppers, and had slept through tryouts. I only lasted one semester there, and Scott and I rarely spoke, but he seemed friendly and genuine and smart, the antithesis of the star athlete stereotype, the kind of guy

Killian Czuba

it's easy to root for. And so I have, ever since.

He went on to be drafted in the third round by the Diamondbacks. I went on to a different junior college. By the time I'd matriculated to an actual university, Scott had made the bigs and was a regular for the Dbacks. In the ensuing years, I watched a lot of baseball — too much, probably, for someone who was supposed to be writing— and I always got a kick out of seeing Scott on my screen. After a successful rookie year, he scuffled through a few seasons with a few organizations as a part-timer, before carving out his current role as a utility and platoon player who specializes in hitting lefties. Scott's the kind of guy often referred to by announcers as a "professional ballplayer," and, for once, that label fits: he's a member of the biggest MLB family ever, one of five Hairstons to play in the pros. He's not a superstar, and he won't make the Hall of Fame, but he's got seven-plus years of service time, millions of dollars in the bank, and at least a few good years left. In a game as fickle as baseball, he's had a hell of a good career.

I've been writing seriously for about as long as Scott's been in the majors. For much of that time, it felt like an esoteric and self-indulgent pursuit; although I sold the book a while ago and have taught writing in various capacities for a decade, I've never felt like a professional anything. But lately, the book's imminent release has prompted thoughts of a career. As a kid, I wanted to be a professional baseball player more than anything in the world; maybe because of that, I don't think of other writers as career benchmarks. I think of ballplayers. Sometimes I think of my former classmate: if I could have a Scott Hairston kind of career, whatever that means in the writing world, I'd count myself lucky.

With two outs, Nationals

JUSTIN ST. GERMAIN

phenom Bryce Harper comes to the plate, a 20-year-old former number-one pick who was on the cover of *Sports Illustrated* at sixteen and looks like he was bred in a lab to play baseball. He's also the biggest jackass in the majors, a player whose early scouting reports called him "a bad, bad guy," an ump-arguing, showboating infant who crafts his horseshit hustling image so painstakingly — pine tar coating his helmet, eye black all over his face, high socks, ratty beard — that he always looks like he's dressed up as himself for Halloween. Harper hits a seeing-eye single through the right side, and when he reaches first base, he tugs theatrically at his batting gloves, jawing with the first base coach. Meanwhile, Hairston scores from second, running straight across home plate and into the dugout, where he slaps a few hands and finds a spot along the dugout railing to watch the rest of the game.

THE BIG E-ZZZZ

HOTEL

NO VACANCY

BURGER KING

BREAKFAST / DRIVE THRU

NOW HIRING

Aaron Alford

SHOELESS JOE WAS A PELICAN
Nicholas Mainieri

My city's NBA team has renamed themselves after a baseball club. The New Orleans Pelicans were established near the end of the Civil War, becoming a professional organization in the 1880s and sticking around through the 1950s as a member of the Southern Association. Shoeless Joe himself, a Pelican, hit a league-leading .354 in 1910. I like to imagine Jackson in darkened saloons, brooding over bourbon and that afternoon's game. He went 3-4, but it is his lone out—a feeble squibber off the fists—that unsettles him.

Demolished a half-century ago, Pelican Stadium stood in Mid-City New Orleans, two blocks from my home (old-time stadiums always existed in neighborhoods), and my house happened to be built the same year Shoeless Joe won the Southern Association batting title. The family who lived here would have seen the ballpark from their porch, grandstand hulking benevolently over rooftops. I can see them gathering their children one summer afternoon to walk down the street, pass through the turnstile, crack open peanuts, and watch Jackson tear around the base paths. How fucking cool would it be, now, if I could sit on the porch in the evening and hear the sounds of the ballpark?

Currently, a little sandlot diamond hides near the space Pelican

Stadium once occupied (the actual location harbors a seedy-looking hotel and Burger King). Sometime last month, I passed this sandlot and saw a group of boys, white and black, playing baseball together. There were no adults, and the kids didn't have uniforms—it had the look and feel of a pickup game. If this kind of scene lives in your imagination, too, then to encounter it in reality might not give you pause.

But how often do you actually witness this sandlot scenario? I'm serious. Give it a moment's thought, as I'm not talking about the organized shit that kids (i.e. their parents) have to pay for. I'm talking about neighborhood children playing baseball together because that's what they want to do and they have a field to do it with. If it isn't almost entirely a figment, then you either live in an unusual place or have lived through a unique time. I drove away before realizing it had been the first neighborhood baseball I'd witnessed at this sandlot since moving to the neighborhood six years ago. I've got to go back to my childhood before I can remember a similar instance at any public diamond, and there aren't many examples there either. I should have pulled over and watched for a bit, if only to prove I hadn't imagined the whole thing, but I was probably in a hurry to get to some goddamn thing I can't even recall.

I began this essay with a mind to introduce my "expert predictions" for the 2014 Major League season, but I've lost myself. Regardless, relative to past years, I know so little about current rosters that I'm embarrassed. Even if my love for baseball never wanes, the amount of attention I pay to the winter transactions of Big League clubs has diminished. I'd need more space and time to investigate why that is, but for starters, it probably suggests that I'm crotchety about contract disputes and the like and will one day become a very annoying older person/baseball fan—if I'm not that already.

However, there is no escaping the fact that the past, both real and imagined, guides the obsessions of all baseball people. You share old stories in the dugout with your teammates; you geek out over statistics important only because of precedent; you sit on the couch, game on, and wax romantic about that throw Clemente once made from the right-field corner.

This year, all I can provide is an exercise in my own nostalgia—and in addition, I meekly offer that when the question concerns the relentless slog of 162 games, nostalgia may yet prove to be more impervious than even expertise.

I'll predict that the Dodgers—whom I once cherished—will meet the Yankees in the World Series (after NY eliminates Boston in a tense, 7-game ALCS), and the Yankees will triumph, ultimately and dramatically, and I'll spend a lot of time thinking about my grandfather preaching the Gospel of DiMaggio to me when I was young.

April 8, 2014 | *BASEBALL, Fiction*

No NO
Kevin Maloney

[Dock] Ellis threw a no-hitter on June 12, 1970. He later stated that he accomplished the feat under the influence of LSD. – Wikipedia

Jerry flashes his fingers between his legs: one-two-three, low and outside. I wind up, pitch and a hundred identical baseballs form a line between my fingers and the jewel in the catcher's mitt. The batter could hit any one of them but he turns into a corkscrew pointing his stick at the sun. The umpire calls a strike or he's the ghost of my grandfather showing me the graves of our ancestors. We're playing the Padres which means "father" in Spanish. You can't fool me; we're babies running around in circles in the kingdom of God.

I roll the orb between my fingers waiting for the next signal but the jewel's too bright. I can't see anything but Jerry's eyes. They're the color of the pills I ate. It's a full

Andrew Shuta

count, 3-2, which are numbers in the alphabet. He blinks which means: pitcher's choice. I throw a curve and Padre swings but the ball's in the bottom of a well a thousand miles deep in my brain. He didn't see that coming.

Padre walks away knocking the bat against his cleats. When he looks into the dugout his brethren hang their heads. I got a no-no going but you don't say "no-no" like you don't step out of an elevator on the 13th floor.

* * *

The next batter is Jimi Hendrix. Jerry flashes two-two-one. That's our sign for, shut the fuck up and just listen to this genius play the guitar.

What the fuck Jerry? This is baseball. I call him to the mound but he doesn't hear me because he's getting Jimi's autograph. Wait, I should get Jimi's autograph too. I look for a pen but all I've got is this baseball. It's enormous. How am I supposed to throw this thing? I throw it and it hits the grass about ten feet in front of Jimi Hendrix and stops before it reaches home plate. Everybody looks at me like I'm on drugs. A drop of rain hits my eyeball and I realize I am on drugs. Jerry tosses me the ball and now it's tiny as a raisin. I don't even need to wind up; I flick it toward home plate like a marble and it hits Jimi Hendrix on the ankle. He walks to first base playing "Foxy Lady" on a Fender Stratocaster.

* * *

What inning is it? How many days did Jesus sit in the desert talking to snakes? My arm has blood in it because my arm's a snake and snakes are full of blood. The batter's full of blood too and the umpire is Richard Nixon. I'm afraid he's going to judge me. All these people are here to judge me and I'm here to be perfect. I got a no-no goin'. I just ate more drugs or maybe I swallowed my gum.

Are you allowed to smoke cigarettes on the pitchers mound? I can't remember. I look to see if I have any cigarettes and then remember I'm playing baseball. All these people are looking at me wondering why I keep touching my pants looking for cigarettes. You shouldn't judge people unless you're on drugs. I'm on drugs and I judge all of you and find you perfect. A no-hitter is when nobody gets to first base off a hit. Second base is feeling under a girl's shirt when you're in middle school.

I look around and realize the bases are loaded. I walked two of these people and hit Jimi Hendrix with a raisin. Jerry flashes three fingers. I hope my arm isn't leaving teeth marks on the ball. I throw it. Padre thinks it's right over the plate but we fooled him by hiding the ball inside another ball. Richard Nixon pumps his fist like he's trying to start a lawn mower. Padre gets angry and throws his bat which is the opposite of religious.

* * *

No No

My teammates say the inning's over. I think I swallowed gum because the drugs aren't stronger. They say only one more inning Dock and I say 'till what? Mazeroski says, you know and I say, the no-no? and he goes, shhhhh! I keep my arm behind my back because I don't want it to bite anybody.

In the dugout I put more gum in my mouth. A bat boy runs his fingers fascinated over the wood grain of a bat. Somebody cut down a tree to make that thing. Jerry sits next to me. His fingers are wrapped in shiny tape. He flexes them, unflexes them, flexes them again. What kind of pitch do you throw when your catcher's fingers look like they just crawled out of the ocean?

The rain picks up. Minnows swim over second base chased by a force darker than baseball. The florescent lights cry out in agony. I'm worried about the ninth. My no-no's a little boat. A baseball is white, stitched together with red yarn. It's so heavy. What's inside this thing? I close my eyes.

Keep talking people, but whatever you do don't say "no-no." I'm on a journey here.

David Kramer

ALL STAR

American League

Topps

CATCHER

MATT NOKES

Samara Pearlstein

April 14, 2014 | *BASEBALL, Nonfiction*

THE FIRST GAME
Nicholas Ward

We parked on Michigan Avenue like we always would, walking hand-in-hand through Corktown, the oldest neighborhood in Detroit. We bought peanuts in brown paper bags from vendors on the street. They were more expensive inside the ballpark but I didn't know that then. "I think these ones taste better," my dad always said.

It was May 1st, 1988. I was in kindergarten, the Detroit Tigers won 98 games the season before, earned an AL East crown, just four years removed from their most-recent World Series victory.

Our seats were down the left field foul line, where my dad had season tickets that he shared with a group of men and their sons. The vendors shouted back and forth across the massive stadium, from left field to right, a call and response hawking "ice cold Cokes!" for no good reason other than it was almost summer and going to be hot soon and there are eighty-two home games a year and time must be passed somehow.

* * *

Tiger Stadium was even then a crumbling masterpiece, all rusted steel and busted concrete, obstructed views from the blue beams that anchored the outfield stands, seats that rose straight up, so you felt close to the action, no matter where you sat.

My dad told me years later that I screamed the whole game, yelling myself hoarse behind this older

109

woman who didn't seem to mind one bit. Matt Nokes, the Tigers promising young catcher, hit two home runs against the Mariners in a come-from-behind victory but I wasn't awake for either of them. I guess I cheered so unrelentingly that I knocked myself to sleep. My dad carried me to the car after the game, like he would all those nights of my childhood, when we were out late visiting relatives and we'd pull into my parents' house in the suburbs, the sound of the garage door jarring me awake in the back seat. "Okay, pal," my dad would say in his home-grown Michigan accent, "we're home."

Other games would leave a mark: missing both of the Cleveland Indians' DH Jim Thome's monster home runs because I was searching for all-star ballots; Cecil Fielder's big blasts that season he hit 51, my aunt Judy visiting from Phoenix, jumping up and down like a little kid because "I just want to see him hit one"; when Ryan Higgins' step-father made us leave early but then we got boxed in on all sides in the parking lot and had to listen to Mickey Tettleton's walk-off, extra-inning shot on the radio while sitting directly outside the stadium.

That first game was before I became the kind of person who remembered all of this, before I collected stacks of baseball cards, before I grew to admire and abhor other franchises, before I realized I loved a game of failure that was destined to break my heart, before I catalogued seasons and players and stats in my brain, filing them away for later, when I will meet others like me, baseball obsessives who romanticize the game beyond all reason, sons and daughters, nieces and nephew, who tell stories of their own games, with fathers and mothers and uncles and aunts and friends, which we collect so we can share, like so many other myths of American life.

It will be a decade, maybe longer, before I realize that continuing to love this game means accepting the sport's tangled history of racism and classism,

NICHOLAS WARD

accepting the wrestling match of corporate greed versus individual greed, accepting an ungodly long regular season followed by a getting-longer-every-year post-season, where the games bookending the year are played by men dressed in winter clothing and paid too much money.

Of course I don't remember the exact day and opponent and box score of that first game. I was six years old, how could I? But I knew Matt Nokes hit two home runs and my dad insisted the game was in early May. A quick search on Baseball Reference finds that Nokes only once hit two homers as a Tiger in early May and that was on May 1st, 1988, a 3-2 victory against the Seattle Mariners. I like being able to pinpoint this. If everything else is memory--where we parked, the peanuts, that it was just the two of us, the crumbling of that masterful stadium--the game is fixed, recorded and set down for all time, exactly .012% of the games the Tigers played at home that season, the season itself just .011% of all years played at Tiger Stadium. A blip. Another day at the ballpark. But if the box score didn't exist, it would be like it never happened and we need validation. See, we get to say, we were there. We remember.

These days Tiger Stadium is just a field on the corner of Michigan and Trumbull. It was demolished and sold for scraps almost five years ago. Despite the steel gates that continue to fortress the area, it's difficult to recall this ground as the hallowed place where the Tigers won four World Series, the last thirty years ago, off a Kirk Gibson bomb in the clinching game; where Cecil knocked his 49th (but not his 50th) that fabled season; where my beloved team finished the second millennium as the worst franchise in baseball. It looks so small now, that patch of land, as if I could get a group of boys together and shag fly balls in the fading afternoon sun. As if I can still hit a baseball. Or know any boys anymore.

April 30, 2014 | *BASEBALL, Nonfiction*

ODE TO JOY
Jim Ruland

People spend their whole lives struggling to get what they think they want, and even if they get it, they find that it's either not what they wanted, or it comes with so many unwanted consequences. We're always shut off from pure joy.

— Harold Ramis

I still can't believe it. Six months after the St. Louis Cardinals put an end to the Los Angeles Dodgers' record-breaking season in the National League Championship, I still can't believe their magical 46-10 run actually happened. Forty-six wins. Ten losses. That's a winning percentage of .821. 46-10 is not a baseball record. It's a college football score — if one of the teams is a Division I powerhouse and the other a backwoods Bible college. They were as invincible a team as I've ever seen play, and I've seen a lot of Dodgers teams over the years, usually with my friend Leo.

I met Leo in the late '90s at an Irish bar on Sunset Boulevard where I used to watch the Knicks back when Patrick Ewing still patrolled the paint. Leo is the most dedicated sports junkie I know with a vast and complicated network of contradictory allegiances. Although he is a hardcore New York sports fan, the Dodgers were his grandmother's team when they were still the Brooklyn Dodgers, and that was

Nick Francis Potter

enough for Leo. Over the years we've gone to dozens of games at Chavez Ravine, but we'd never seen a run like this.

What made it so remarkable was how badly the season began. When Hanley Ramirez was injured in the World Baseball Classic, Justin Sellers, who stands 5'10 and weighs 160 pounds, filled in for him at shortstop. Then Juan Uribe missed time at third base and manager Don Mattingly was forced to go to Luis Cruz. Justin Sellers batted .188, striking out 20 times in just 69 at bats; but those numbers were good compared Cruz's, whose batting average was a pitiful .127. A clip of Sellers rolling an imaginary blunt (to go with his imaginary production at the plate) pretty much summarizes that experiment.

You could say injuries prevented Mattingly from fielding a competitive team.

You could say the Dodgers underperformed.

You could say they flat out sucked.

Things were looking bleak for the boys in blue. The Dodgers began the month of May with an eight-game losing streak and opened June ranked 20th in on-base percentage and 28th in runs scored. The pitching staff wasn't getting any run support and closer Brandon League was pitching like he was getting paid for blowing saves. Then disaster struck. Outfielders Matt Kemp and Carl Crawford injured their hamstrings in the same week, forcing the Dodgers to call up Yasiel Puig, the 22-year-old prospect whose defection from Cuba in 2012 was so harrowing the rights to the story have been acquired by Hollywood.

Puig signed a contract for $42 million and batted a blistering .526 in spring training; but in 40 games of Double-A ball had averaged "only" .313 with eight home runs, 37 RBIs and a .982 OPS. These are good numbers, but it wasn't the kind of performance that made anyone in the Dodger organization think they could throw Puig into the line-up and ask him to carry the team. That's exactly what the Dodgers did and Puig responded.

In his first game as a major leaguer, Puig went 2-4 against the Padres, but it was a play with his arm that got everyone's attention. In the top of the ninth he one-handed a deep fly ball and gunned down a base runner with a game-ending double play.

* * *

If I'm not at the ballpark, I prefer to listen to the broadcasts via the MLB app, which is the best $20 a baseball fan can spend. Vin Scully calls the first three innings, which is enough (there, I said it) and then he turns it over to Charlie Steiner and Rick Monday. The game of baseball is a narrative in numbers. It's great radio but terrible television. But Puig changed all that. I needed to see this player with the once-in-a-generation skill set. When he threw that laser to Adrian Gonzales to double up Chris Denorfia, all the Dodger fans in the bar stood up and gave each other high fives with stunned expressions on their faces as if to say, Did you see that? Did that actually happen?

The next day Puig hit two home runs and drove in five RBI. Two days later, a grand slam. The day after, another dinger. In his first 15 games he racked up 27 hits. Nearly every day in June Puig tied or surpassed a new team or league record. He closed out the month with 44 hits, the most ever by a Dodger rookie and the second most in league history – and Puig didn't even play the entire month. Who knows, with those extra days he might have even caught up to the guy who held the record: Joe DiMaggio.

This is when baseball purists began to lose it. They were outraged that someone who'd been in the league for less than a month was being compared to DiMaggio. In L.A. it was a different story. Puig fever gripped the city. You could turn on any radio station and hear the chatter. It was all Puig all the time. While the rest of the country was still trying to figure out how to pronounce his name, "Viva Puig" and "MVPuig" had become the city's mantras.

I was no exception. I don't drink anymore, but I started going to bars to watch Puig play. He is that rare player who passes the eyeball test: he is bigger, faster and quicker than anyone else on the diamond. He looks more like a linebacker than an outfielder. My interest in Puig crossed over to infatuation on June 11, when he was grazed on the nose by an inside pitch, setting off a series of retaliatory strikes that led to starting pitcher Zack Greinke getting beaned. A melee ensued and Puig lustily threw himself into the fray.

The next day, radio personality Petros Papadakis of the Petros and Money show on AM 570, the Dodgers flagship radio station in Los Angeles, broke down the skirmish and identified audio from the dust-up as belonging to Puig. "Yo soy Cubano! I am not afraid!" he shouted.

"Yo soy Cubano!" became the show's oft-repeated refrain for the rest of the week and it worked its way into my own lingo, too. I taunted coworkers, trolled my wife. It was my go-to response whenever the veracity of an assertion was called into question, even though I am 1) not Cuban 2) full of fear. I was such a fan boy that I would have bought a Yasiel Puig lunchbox if there had been one to buy, but there wasn't, so I made one of my own.

"Admit it," my wife said. "You love him."

Although I suspected she was jealous, because it was a most excellent lunch box, there was no point in denying the truth.

"Yo soy Cubano. I am not afraid."

JIM RULAND

* * *

As amazing as it was to watch the emergence of a bona fide superstar, Puig's heroics did not lift the Dodgers out of their doldrums. On June 21, the team's record with Puig in the line-up was a dismal 7-10.

I finally had a chance to see Puig with my own eyes at Petco Park in San Diego. Leo was going to take the train down from L.A. and spend a day with me at the ballpark; but at the last minute he had to cancel because his knee, which he'd injured in a skiing accident a long time ago and had never healed properly, was giving him problems and wasn't getting better.

I didn't have tickets. It was the third game of a four-game series and the Dodgers had dropped the first two. The Dodgers were 30-42, a woeful 9.5 games out of first place. Zack Greinke was pitching against San Diego for the first time since he was injured in a benches-clearing brawl with the team back in April. I worried that it would be a less-than-family-friendly environment for my daughter, who was nine years old at the time.

At the last minute, we decided to go. I paid too much for a pair of tickets and a bowl of nachos, and we were treated to a 6-1 victory. We didn't know it yet, but it was the beginning of the Dodgers record-smashing run. The Dodgers would go on to win six games in a row, take 10 out of 11, 16 out of the next 19, etc. Their run coincided with some atrocious baseball by the rest of the division and the Dodgers shot up the standings. Exactly one month after that game in San Diego they'd erased a ten-game deficit and were atop the division.

At the end of July, I splurged on a set of four tickets and got some friends together to see the Dodgers face the New York Yankees in what would be Mariano Rivera's last game at Dodgers Stadium. Although Leo's knee was still giving him fits – he was finally getting the physical therapy he'd put off for so many years – he assured me he would be there.

When we met up for the game, it was clear his condition was worse than he'd let on. In spite of aggressive rehabilitation, his knee wasn't getting better. If anything it was worse. He'd just come from the acupuncturist and his knee had locked up. He said it would loosen up, but couldn't say when. He warned me that he had to go slow and that it would take him a long time to get to our seats, which were in the upper deck. I asked him what was causing his knee to flare up like this.

"That's just it," he told me. "They don't know."

Leo wasn't joking about going slow. It took him forever just to get across the parking lot. I'd walk with my friends for a bit and then we'd wait for him to catch up. He kept urging us to go on without him, which I couldn't bring myself to do.

Finally my friends went ahead to claim our seats and buy hot dogs and beer. Before we even got inside the park, ushers were offering Leo a wheelchair, which he brushed off. I didn't blame him, but the way he was staggering around like a sailor on shore leave, I was worried someone would think he was intoxicated and start some trouble. It wasn't just that his leg was stiff and his gait was slow, but his balance was off as well.

The Dodgers were down 0-3 in the ninth inning and Mariano Rivera trotted out for the save. They even played "Enter Sandman" for him. We all agreed that it would have been nice if the Dodgers had won, but it was better to have witnessed history. "Fuck yeah it was," Leo said. I wasn't so sure.

* * *

The Dodgers continued their historic march into the record books. They finished the season 92-70 with an eleven-game lead in the division.

With the playoffs locked up, the critics zeroed in on Puig and the steady decline of his batting average. As Puig's numbers went down, so did Leo's health. Actually, that's not true. Leo's health – his knee in particular – stayed the same; it's the diagnoses that kept getting worse.

He had a team of doctors working on him now. They began to suspect that he was experiencing nerve damage and that the cause might be neurological. One thought it was MS – multiple sclerosis. Another thought it could be a brain tumor. Yet another doctor didn't want to rule out Lyme disease. Except the doctors never definitely said this or that; they said it might be this or it could be that. Leo underwent an arsenal of invasive tests and scans to rule out each calamity. It was maddening and expensive. The weight of not knowing was getting him down.

The moment playoff tickets went on sale I jumped online and bought a pair to Game 3 against the Atlanta Braves. The Dodgers had lost Game 2 after winning the opener. There was no question as to whom I would take.

I drove up from San Diego but got stuck in traffic and was running late to meet up with Leo. If we didn't hustle, we'd miss the first pitch. Of course, Leo wasn't hustling anywhere. When I got in his car to drive up to the stadium, he had more bad news.

"They sent me to a new doctor. He says I've got ALS."

"But that's...."

"A death sentence."

I was going to say "Lou Gehrig's disease," but same difference. As we picked our way across the parking lot, I studied my friend's walk more carefully to see if his uncertain gait had atrophied, but I detected no change. I went slower this time. Our seats were in right field so we had farther to walk, but we were in no hurry. Every so often ushers would appear from nowhere to offer their assistance, experts in what I had been blind to see: my friend was not well.

The rookie pitcher, Hyun-jin Ryu, gave up two runs in the first. By the time we made it to our seats the Dodgers were down and whatever electricity the fans in the ballpark had whipped up had now fizzled away. I went through all the things I knew about ALS. The speed with which it manifests, the severity of its symptoms. In sports, we like to think of the playoffs as do or die situations, win or go home. But now that death was in the cards for Leo, that comparison felt trite. I couldn't stop myself from wondering if this was the last game I was going to see with my friend.

Leo's news, however, did not diminish the importance of the game, at least not in my mind. Just the opposite in fact. If life is finite and fleeting, and we know that it is, then the pursuit of perfection in one specific thing makes a lot more sense than the random, purposeless mess that we generally make of things. It's the pursuit that's ennobling, not the achievement, and no entity on this earth does a better job of documenting that pursuit than baseball. It is a place where everything can be known and nothing is arbitrary. An umpire may blow a call, a pitcher may miss the strike zone, a ball may come *this* close to leaving the park, but almost no one dies playing baseball and if death were somehow part of the game, believe me, they'd get the fucking diagnosis right the first time. When time is not on your side, the best place to be is at a game with no clock.

Our seats were excellent. It was a gorgeous evening. Beach balls tumbled in the air as if in a dream. In the bottom of the second, a Dodger got on base. Then another. The woman sitting next to me slapped my leg and then apologized for getting carried away. Strangers exchanged ferocious high fives as the tension kept climbing higher and higher.

JIM RULAND

Then it happened.

Carl Crawford lifted a high fly ball way up in the azure sky for a no-doubt-about-it home run, and hung there in the air for long enough to change everything. It was the strangest thing. The volume got so loud that it transcended the audible realm and enlisted other senses. Our bodies shook, but we were absolutely still. Speech wasn't possible yet we were all in communication with each other. It was grand, it was glorious, and we were all witnesses to something extraordinary. There was no me, no Leo, no other people. No boundaries whatsoever. My heart desired to speak. My eyes wanted to sing. I believe the name for this feeling is joy.

The Dodgers scored four runs in the second inning, two in the third, and four more in the fourth and won 13-6. Puig went 3-5. The Braves went home defeated and demoralized. They had received their diagnosis and the outlook wasn't good.

The Dodgers advanced to the National League Championship and were eliminated in six games by the St. Louis Cardinals, who lost to the Boston Red Sox in the World Series, though it was hard to care. It was football season, after all, and I had wagers to lose, fantasy teams to mismanage, entire Sundays to piss away while Leo underwent more tests.

His team was incensed with the new doctor's diagnosis and set out to find out what was wrong with Leo for once and for all. In the parlance of medical professionals, they ripped the doctor a new one. Their anger was justified when the final, ironclad diagnosis came in: Leo did not have ALS; he had MS. There isn't a cure but the symptoms are treatable and they are making great strides, which is what they always say, but still.

Leo sent me the good news in a text: "Looks like I'll be around for another season after all."

SEAMS
Jill Talbot

When I think back on it, it's a couple of seconds, a rush from the plate to the mound, a flash, a gasp, and my grip on my father's arm. It was August 4, 1993, and we watched from a high-up section of washed-out-blue seats, lounging the afternoon game when Ventura tossed his bat and helmet and started running. Dad and I on our feet as fast as Ryan's punches. Players from both benches spilled onto the field like starlings in flight.

My grandfather was an All-State pitcher in Texas for McKinney High School in the early 1920s. I have a sepia photograph of him in a Pillbox ball cap with an "M" on it. When his team won the state championship

his senior year, he had offers from both St. Louis and Detroit. But after graduation, he attended Perkins School of Theology at Southern Methodist University, and until the early 1970s, he served churches in North Texas—Electra, Bowie, Dallas, Gainesville. He liked to say he chose the Lord over baseball.

In 1950, my father went to Stephen F. Austin University in Nacogdoches, Texas on a football scholarship, but during the summers, he played baseball for Martinsville. He said the team had a nice stadium outside of town. Several surrounding towns also had teams, and they'd play three or four games a week. My father

Aaron Alford

123

center field. Once, a manager and a coach from another team showed up at a game and offered him cash to play for them. My father told them no, he couldn't do that.

I was in fifth grade when some of the kids at PE started playing baseball in a dirt field. I wandered over to stand in line for my turn to bat, and I went back every day until I got a chance to pitch. When that chance came, I threw the ball to one batter after another until the teacher's whistle called us away. I kicked at the dirt—marking my mound so I could find it the next day. After a couple of weeks, the other team dragged onto the makeshift field and wouldn't line up. They complained no one ever got on base.

I found the video of the Ryan/Ventura fight on MLB.com. Nolan Ryan steps back, one, two. Then his knee flicks up as quick as a dancer's on a count. The clip runs for six minutes and twenty-six seconds—much longer than the rush of my recollection. Ryan staggers out from beneath the heap buttoning his jersey, and Ventura paces in a daze. The announcer's surprise: "Look at this." The deep blue seats of the stands challenge the fade of my memory, and it looks like the game is being played at night. But the sun I remember. The suddenness I remember.

My father was a freshmen in high school when my grandfather was preaching in Bowie, a small town ninety miles northwest of Dallas. My father third baseman. One day, my grandfather came to practice and the coach asked him to pitch. "He pitches two innings in his street clothes," (my Dad likes to tell this one), "no one got a hit off him."

My grandfather retired shortly after I was born in 1970, so I never got to see him preach, but when I'd visit during the season, he'd have a game on as loud as it would go. I like to keep a baseball game on in my house. Just to hear it.

At the age of eighty, my father still announces the high school baseball games at Tillery Field in Mesquite, Texas. He takes his CD player to the press box to play songs between innings. I've never been to one of those games, but I'm sure every player on the roster knows "Wipe Out," "Whole Lotta Shakin' Goin' On," and "Jailhouse Rock."

Just after college, I almost married a guy who loved sports probably more than he loved me. One day he showed up at my apartment with two gloves and a ball. "Here," he said, coming toward me while I slid the glove over my hand and fingered the ball, "let me show you how to hold it." Then he stopped and looked at my hand. I

did, too, amazed by the way it formed with an instinct I didn't know I had. The seams beneath my fingers sure. We tossed the ball until we squinted against the dusk to see it. When what I threw thwacked against his glove, I could feel it.

When my father was playing baseball those college summers, some of the fans would pitch in two bucks for each home run he hit. After the game, they'd hand him the collection through the fence. He remembers Murray Shaw, the catcher, and Bobby Flanagan, second base, the way the three of them were offered contracts to play in the Major League Baseball rookie league in Florida. The way they were told they'd maybe move up. "I was a junior then. I didn't take their offer," (he likes to tell this one, too), "I wanted to play football another year. I wanted to finish college and become a coach." He did.

I don't remember much about that Rangers and White Sox afternoon except Ventura's rush to the mound. In October of that same year, the Rangers played their last game in Arlington Stadium. Now they play at Globe Life Park, and my father and I still make a game or two every season. He gets peanuts. We share a Diet Dr. Pepper. I grip his arm when we stand and cheer for home runs. When we wander out to the parking lot, he likes to remind me we're walking where the old stadium used to be.

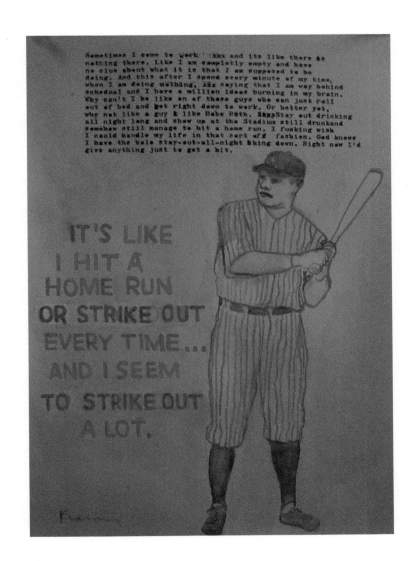

IT'S LIKE
I HIT A
HOME RUN
OR STRIKE OUT
EVERY TIME...
AND I SEEM
TO STRIKE OUT
A LOT.

Sometimes I come to work Xxx and its like there is
nothing there. Like I am completly empty and have
no clue about what it is that I am supposed to be
doing. And this after I spend every minute of my time,
when I am doing nothing, xxx saying that I am way behind
schedual and I have a million ideas burning in my brain.
Why can't I be like on of these guys who can just roll
out of bed and get right down to work. Or better yet,
why not like a guy k like Babe Ruth. XxxxStay out drinking
all night long and show up at the Stadium still drunkand
somehow still manage to hit a home run. I fucking wish
I could handle my life in that sort off fashion. God knows
I have the hole stay-out-all-night bking down. Right now I'd
give anything just to get a hit.

David Kramer

CONTRIBUTORS

Aaron Alford's (illustrations, pp. 64, 98, & 122) writing has appeared in *Oxford American, Memoir, Hobart* online, *Bellingham Review, River Teeth, The Los Angeles Review*, and elsewhere. He earned a Ph.D. in Literature and Creative Writing at Texas Tech University and now serves as Managing Editor of *Southern Humanities Review*. He lives in Auburn, Alabama, with his wife, who says it's okay if he gets a tattoo of the Astrodome, and his two sons, who have not yet learned to talk but are already taller than Jose Altuve. Find him online at aaronalford.com.

*

Sam Anderson-Ramos ("Baseball is Poetry," p. 63) is a novelist, short story writer, and essayist. His work has appeared in numerous publications including *The Chicago Tribune Printers Row Journal* and *The Austin Chronicle*. He has been a Lecturer in art and writing at The School of the Art Institute of Chicago and an Adjunct Professor of writing at St. Augustine College. He lives in Chicago but will be returning soon to his hometown, Austin, Texas.

Baseball is beautiful, in part, because of its timelessness. So while my life has changed significantly since this piece was published, and while any baseball team is constantly shuffling players in and out, the Astros are still my Astros, and baseball is still baseball, no matter one's age, or where it's being played. That's what this story is about.

*

Andrew Bomback ("I've Got Dreams to Remember," p. 41) is a physician and writer in New York. His stories and essays have recently appeared or are forthcoming in *The Kenyon Review, Human Parts, Hobart, Harlequin, Palaver, For Every Year, Full Grown People, SmokeLong Quarterly, Diagram, Elysian Fields Quarterly, Bellevue Literary Review, Westchester Review*, and *Essay Daily*. He is the author of *You're Too Wonderful to Die*, a novel, and *Chronic Kidney Disease and Hypertension Essentials*, a textbook.

I wrote this story more than seven years ago, when I still wrote short stories, the Mets were a respectable team, and I was naive enough to think that just saying in October "maybe we should try getting pregnant now" could automatically translate into a summertime baby. Since this piece came out, I abandoned fiction (both writing it and reading it), the Mets became the laughing stock of Major League Baseball, and my wife and I struggled with three years of "unexplained infertility." However, another way to look at things, the "Ya Gotta Believe!" way of looking at things: In those seven years, I became a nonfiction convert, Johan Santana tossed the first and only Mets no-hitter, and I had a daughter and son who attended their first Mets game this year. I prefer the second version. I took the title of "I've Got Dreams to Remember" from an Otis Redding song, but the inspiration behind this story was actually another song, "Listening to Otis Redding at Home During Christmas" by Okkervil River. I've always loved that Okkervil River song's chorus, which is essentially a re-interpretation of "I've Got Dreams to Remember." This story was an attempt at my own reinvention of that song. It's a treat for me to re-read it now, because it reminds me of my own dreams from that time, some of which have fortunately come true.

*

Killian Czuba (illustrations, pp. 74 & 95) writes words and draws pictures. She is the Art Director and a writing contributor to *Barrelhouse*, and the founder/"Ideas Man" of ApiaryLife.org. She's published comics, illustrations, and prose fiction, but most often publishes tweets + podcasts. Follow her @killianczuba.

*

Timothy Denevi's ("The Wolfman in Barry Bonds," p. 29) first book is *Hyper*. He lives near Washington, DC and is a faculty member in George Mason University's MFA program, where he teaches nonfiction.

On the night during which the events of this essay took place—August 8th, 2003—San Francisco beat Philadelphia 9-1. I'd just turned twenty four, and before the game that evening, my father (bless him) had organized a visit to the clubhouse via his friend John Yandle, a batting practice pitcher for the team and also a close friend of Bonds's—the sort of birthday present you might hope for as a ten-year-old boy. But at that specific time in my life, just out of college, I was working as a middle-school teacher in Honolulu (I'd flown back home that week to visit family in San Jose) and in retrospect you could say that my lifelong fandom for the Giants was made acute by my newfound geographical isolation, to the point where I'd managed to conflate a general sense of homesickness toward the Bay Area with the sports team representing it—specifically, with the best player on that team, a man who off the field was known to be surly and short-tempered but who, in the batter's box, had come to display a degree of patience that, despite his subsequently confirmed steroid use, resembled something that bordered on the preternatural.

*

Elizabeth Ellen ("Priceless," p. 12) is the author of *Fast Machine* (SF/LD).

"Priceless" was one of the first nonfiction stories I wrote. I hadn't been writing too long at this point. Or maybe I am just feeling embarrassed by the cheesiness of the story; by the unabashed sentimentality with which I wrote it. I read it aloud to my daughter this morning. She is 19 now. She just finished her first year of college. She said, "Did you

131

fictionalize that? I don't remember half of that happening." She said, "Please tell me it's not called 'priceless.'" I laughed. Of course it's called 'priceless.'

I took my daughter to a baseball game on Mother's Day this year. I guess it was the first game we went to—just the two of us—since the game I wrote about in 'Priceless.' It rained off and on throughout the game and we ended up leaving during the rain delay at the end. We ate pizza using a garbage can as a table and found a new photograph of her great-great grandfather in the Tigers' memorabilia case and picked a new favorite baseball player—J. D. Martinez—because he was cute and tall and had a good walk up song (Rick Ross's "Hustlin").

"What I remember most of that game is you saying, 'We're independent women because we came to a baseball game by ourselves,'" my daughter just told me, smiling.

"I did?" I said. I hadn't remembered.

My daughter is an independent, young adult woman now. My daughter is my best friend now. She probably has been for nineteen years.

It's still hard not to write sentimentally about her, about 'us.' I would be tempted to title every story about her/us, "Priceless." And they would all be worthy of that title.

T.S. Flynn ("Predictions," p. 81) is an educator and writer in Minneapolis who blogs at It's a long season (mightyflynn.tumblr.com) and tweets from @mighty_flynn. When he's not teaching, tumbling, or tweeting, he's slowly writing a book about his great-great uncle Tom Sheehan's sixty-five year career in baseball.

I wrote "Predictions" near the end of the worst of eight Minnesota winters I've known. Every morning I walked in darkness through a rail yard and industrial zone to catch my bus to work. I perfected a Herb Brooks ice-shuffle that winter, but still fell hard five times. My first tumble resulted in a concussion, the fourth in a severely sprained wrist. The snow melted in mid-March but gravity struck again when I tripped on a broken sidewalk while walking with a friend. Trying to avoid re-injuring my sprained right wrist, I landed awkwardly and broke my left wrist. So I wrote "Predictions" under the influence of Percocet while wearing a cast. As always, baseball couldn't arrive soon enough. But I'd also been thinking about 1993 a lot as the season approached because it would be the Colorado Rockies' twentieth. Denver is my hometown, and I'd spent my life wishing and then waiting for Major League Baseball to arrive in the Mountain Time Zone, so I started the sketches that would become "Predictions" by writing about Eric Young's Opening Day lead-off home run. After that, a daisy-chain of memories unraveled and I tried to describe what I can still remember of all those moments in ballparks.

Following "Predictions," I "predicted" the 2013 divisional standings. Really, it should have been titled, "How I Hope 2013 Shakes Out." Two of the teams I picked to win divisions—the White Sox and Blue Jays—finished in last place, and none of my other divisional champs finished first. I was 0 for 6. Baseball is a game of failure.

*

Tod Goldberg ("Joltin' Joe Has Left and Gone Away," p. 21) is the author of over a dozen books, including, most recently, *Gangsterland*. His essay "When They Let Them Bleed," which first appeared in *Hobart*, was selected for *Best American Essays 2013*. He lives in Indio, CA where he directs the Low Residency MFA in Creative Writing & Writing for the Performing Arts at the University of California, Riverside.

What I remember most about writing "Joltin' Joe Has Left and Gone Away"—ten years ago now—is how angry I was. I didn't love my father, because I barely knew him, and in the years since, that hasn't changed. What has, however, is my appreciation for the small things we inherit in this life, the meditative calm I find in watching baseball by myself—as I'm doing right now, midnight in late spring, my wife and dog asleep on the bed, the Oakland A's about to lose to the Chicago White Sox, though the A's don't know it yet because they don't have MLB Extra Innings – and that reminds me of a detail I left out of this essay. My father, when he died, was sitting up, eating a pizza, and watching

133

the Mariners play the Angels. I know that he was having a difficult time in his life then, that he was unhappy, and so I can see him trying to lose himself in the game for a few hours. The Mariners lost by one that night. They were down two runs going into the 8th and they scored three runs that inning, only to have the Angels come back and drop two on them in the bottom of the 8th. I don't know if my father was still alive by then and maybe ten years ago, I would have hoped that he was, that he would have had that final disappointment, but I'm not that person anymore, and so now I hope he saw them rally and take the lead, that he died thinking his team had won.

*

Katie Gross (illustrations, pp. 46 & 86) is originally from Philadelphia, now resides in Long Island City, Queens and is succumbing to the fandom of her local New York Mets. She has obtained a degree in illustration from Parsons School of Design with a focus in printmaking and is continuing her studies at Parsons pursuing her masters in History of Design and Curatorial Studies.

*

David Kramer (illustrations, pp. 3, 45, 107, & 127) was born in New York City where he currently lives and works. A fan of all New York teams, Kramer came of age as a sports fan watching the 1977 and '78 Yankees. Thurman Munson being the player he most identified with...Kramer's work has been shown throughout North America and Europe. His videos recently were included in Stand/Up at the Muse du Pompidou in Paris. His show, Kramerica! opens at Galerie Tanit in Munich in September 2015.

*

Alice Lowe ("Seventh Inning Stretch," p. 47) reads and writes about food and family, Virginia Woolf, and life. Her personal essays have appeared in numerous literary journals, including *Permafrost, Labletter, Upstreet, Hippocampus, Tinge, Switchback*, and

Prime Number. She was the 2013 national award winner at City Works Journal and winner of a 2011 essay contest at Writing It Real. Work on Virginia Woolf includes two monographs published by Cecil Woolf Publishers in London, *Virginia Woolf as Memoirst* in 2015 and *Beyond the Icon: Virginia Woolf in Contemporary Fiction* in 2010. Alice lives in San Diego, California and blogs at www.aliceloweblogs.wordpress.com.

I'm told that we writers are not supposed to like our early work. It's an embarrassment now that we're so polished, published and prolific, right? Yet I have to confess that "Seventh Inning Stretch" remains one of my favorite pieces. Not only was it the first personal essay I had accepted for publication after I launched my late-blooming writing career, but it never fails to bring up fond baseball-hued memories that touch on four generations of my family, from my mother to my grandson, with homage to literary touchstones Jane Austen and Virginia Woolf thrown in for good measure.

The Padres are still my home team, but my heart remains true to the Yankees. My two teams met in San Diego in 2013—the first time since 2002—and at least half the crowd was wearing pinstripes, including me. The Padres dominated this time, unlike previous meetings. Oh well, waddaya gonna do?

*

Ben Lyon ("The Day the Music Should Have Died," p. 57) is a lawyer living in Chicago and has been published in *The Classical* and *Pitchers & Poets*. He also commits minor NCAA infractions as @bblyon on Twitter.

After reading this again, I'm reminded of the epic rant Chris Rock recently gave on "Real Sports" about baseball and African-Americans, which hits at some of the points I tried to make in this essay about baseball looking to the future instead of the past. (So what I'm saying is, basically, I'm better than one of the greatest comics of this generation and HBO owes *Hobart* some serious $$.)

With that in mind, I recently Googled some images of the 1979 World Series and found glorious pics of yellow Pirate pullovers matched up against Cheetos-orange O's uniforms, and it seemed more like the future than any baseball game I've seen this year. Meaning we *still* need to look to the past to get the future the sport deserves. I suggest we start by re-introducing pullover jerseys and then *maybe*, if we're feeling super confident, the bullpen car. (Oh and speaking of the Koch brothers, it's a good thing they're not around to ruin American democracy anymore (silently weeps into a high school Civics textbook).)

I'd like to end by noting that my father and uncle got into an argument about this piece immediately after reading it, which is the most proud I've been of my family this decade, and maybe illustrates more perfectly than anything I've written thus far that the past is the future; the future is the past.

*

Nicholas Mainieri ("Shoeless Joe Was a Pelican," p. 99) is a frequent contributor to the annual baseball issue at *Hobart* online. His work has appeared among various literary publications, including the *Southern Review, the Southern Humanities Review, Midwestern Gothic,* and *Sou'wester.* He holds an MFA from the University of New Orleans and a BA from the University of Notre Dame, where he also played baseball. He grew up in Florida, Colorado, and Indiana, though he now calls New Orleans home.

"Shoeless Joe Was a Pelican" began as a highfalutin introduction to whatever my predictions for the 2014 Major League season were going to be, but I got stuck waxing romantic about things I never witnessed—always dangerous. I became more interested in the baseball Pelicans of New Orleans after the Hornets rebranded themselves as an homage, and it was a cool discovery to learn that Joe Jackson had his best days as a Pelican the same year my home was built two blocks from his batter's box. We tend to think of baseball as having bucolic origins, but I believe it is more accurate to say that baseball evolved in the city as necessary opposition to the rigidity of urban life and defined workdays. By now, however, baseball has largely moved out of city centers. The

New Orleans Zephyrs, our current Triple-A team, play in the concrete wasteland near the airport, half an hour outside of town. There are exceptions, but new professional stadiums require lots of parking and public diamonds cost cash-strapped cities too much to maintain. There are many factors behind the diminishing interest in baseball among American children, but the near impossibility of finding a regular pick-up game doesn't help. The hope kindled in witnessing just a couple at-bats of that one pick-up game in Mid-City, New Orleans was significant, and still a frequent comfort.

*

Kevin Maloney ("No No," p. 103) is a writer living in Portland, Oregon. His debut novel *Cult of Loretta* was published by Lazy Fascist Press in May 2015. His stories have appeared in *PANK*, *Monkeybicycle*, and *Pamplemousse*. Find more at kevinmaloney.net.

I enjoy writing about drugs. It doesn't matter which one. "Drugs" is just an excuse for me, as a prose writer, to become a poet. This is particularly true when a first-person narrator takes a pill or smokes something or snorts a line. It's like turning the page of a Raymond Carver story and finding yourself in the second half of Naked Lunch. The ordinary becomes extraordinary. Metaphors are no longer symbolic, but actual hallucinations. In the case of "No No," the only sober moment is a two sentence epigraph introducing the legend of Dock Ellis. From there, the reader is immediately plunged into Dock's inebriated brain. The narrative details come from this quote I found on Wikipedia:

> The ball was small sometimes, the ball was large sometimes, sometimes I saw the catcher, sometimes I didn't. ...I started having a crazy idea in the fourth inning that Richard Nixon was the home plate umpire, and once I thought I was pitching a baseball to Jimi Hendrix, who to me was holding a guitar and swinging it over the plate.

Everything else I made up. The comic tone of the story comes from my attempt at ripping off Denis Johnson's *Jesus' Son*... particularly the ending of "Car Crash While Hitchhiking."

*

Eric Nusbaum's ("The Umpire," p. 69) fiction has appeared in *Bluestem, elimae, Hobart,* and *Needle*. His nonfiction has appeared in *Sports Illustrated, ESPN the Magazine, Slate, Gawker,* and *The Best American Sports Writing*. He is an editor at *VICE*.

This story is very clearly umpire fan fiction (or maybe historical fiction?). I wrote it a short time after umpire Jim Joyce blew a call at first base, and cost Detroit Tigers pitcher Armando Galarraga a perfect game on the final out. Galarraga was a journeyman pitcher, and the near-perfect game was the highlight of his career. Joyce, on the other hand, was and remains one of baseball's most well-respected umpires. Afterwards, Galarraga was almost saintly in his benevolence. Joyce apologized and Galarraga gave him a hug. I couldn't help but wonder how an umpire might deal with that -- how the accumulation of thousands of judgments made over a lonely career spent constantly traveling might affect his outlook.

*

Whitney Pastorek ("Baseball Messiah," p. 5) is a writer, photographer, and international star of stage and screen whose work has appeared in the *New York Times, Sports Illustrated, ESPN the Magazine, Details, the Village Voice,* and *Fast Company,* among many others. She was a writer on staff at *Entertainment Weekly* for six years, the editor of a literary magazine called *Pindeldyboz* for over a decade, and has spent the past 5 years engaged in an immersive anthropological field study of the country music industry.

I originally wrote the first version of this piece for the *American Journal of Print*'s 2001 Autumn/Winter edition. *Hobart* excerpted this version some time later (2003?), and what's funny is the bit it leaves out: the bit in between the two versions.

I mention at the end of the piece that I'd become a fan of the Yankees since moving to NYC. I do not mention, however, that in the Autumn/Winter of 2001, I spent nearly every single day watching the Yankees play baseball. I was in Yankee Stadium on September 10, 2001, for a game that got rained out. I was in Yankee Stadium on September 25, 2001, the first game back, the night the Yanks clinched the division. I was in Yankee Stadium on October 31, 2001, as extra innings stretched past midnight, and Derek Jeter became Mr. November. I was in a bar in Queens when Mo blew the save in Game 7, and the Diamondbacks proved to me once and for all that I am not, in fact, the Baseball Messiah.

It doesn't matter. Nothing that's happened in the past 12 years—and I could tell you some stories—has changed the fact that I freakin' love baseball. I'm writing this from my new home in Nashville, TN, trying to slam some words onto metaphorical paper before dashing out the door to watch the Nashville Sounds play the New Orleans Zephyrs at this city's gorgeous new minor league ballpark. I'm not overly invested, but I'd like the Sounds to win. And if they do, I hope there will be a kid in the stands who thinks they had something to do with it.

*

Samara Pearlstein (illustrations, pp. 4, 40, 80, 108) works with systems of information, examining these systems and the frameworks used to render them intelligible through the lens of drawing. (Baseball is a particularly wonderful system of information, with particularly wonderful information-organizing frameworks.) Samara received a BFA from the University of Michigan, and an MFA from the School of the Museum of Fine Arts, Boston/Tufts University.

Nick Francis Potter (illustrations, pp. 0, 56, 68) is the author of *New Animals* (Subito Press). He currently lives in Missouri with his wife and two boys.

Jarod Roselló (illustrations, pp. 14, 15, 19, 20, 35) is a Cuban-American cartoonist, writer, and teacher from Miami, Florida. His debut graphic novel, *The Well-Dressed Bear Will (Never) Be Found* is forthcoming August 2015 from Publishing Genius Press and his serialized comic, "Those Bears," can be read online at *Hobart*. He teaches comics and fiction in the creative writing program at University of South Florida.

Jim Ruland ("Ode to Joy," p. 113) is the author of *Forest of Fortune* and *Big Lonesome*. He is currently collaborating with Keith Morris of Black Flag, Circle Jerks and OFF! about his life in punk rock. Jim is the curator of the longstanding SoCal-based reading series Vermin on the Mount.

"Ode to Joy" was written in the months after the 2013 baseball season and before the 2014 campaign began. Not much has changed since then – the Dodgers lost to the Cardinals (again) and my friend's condition remains more or less the same, which is good in the sense that his health hasn't deteriorated further. There are, however, reasons for hope. The Dodgers have beefed up their bullpen and their re-investment in their farm system is starting to pay dividends with Joc Pederson tearing the cover of the ball and more prospects waiting to be called up. Leo is fighting MS with medication, physical therapy, and daily yoga. He is hopeful that he will be approved for stem cell treatments and reverse the slow degeneration of the nervous system to which most

MS sufferers eventually succumb. One of the humbling things about baseball is that every event that transpires on the field is tallied and recorded. How can one person make a difference in a universe where the same plays happen over and over again with maddening regularity? It sometimes feels as if there are as many hits and pitches in the baseball atlas as there are stars in the sky, yet every year someone does something that's never been done before. Maybe this year that someone will be Leo.

*

Devan Sagliani ("All My Childhood Heroes Played Ball," p. 33) was born and raised in Southern California and graduated from UCLA. He is the author of the *Zombie Attack* series, *The Rising Dead, A Thirst For Fire*, and the *Undead L.A.* series. Devan also wrote the original screenplay for the movie *HVZ: Humans Versus Zombies*. He writes a bimonthly horror column for *Escapist Magazine* called Dark Dreams. In 2014 he cofounded the At Hell's Gates horror anthology series with Shana Festa, which donates all proceeds to The Intrepid Fallen Heroes Fund to help wounded soldiers and their families.

Devan is an active member of the Horror Writer's Association. His fiction has been nominated for the Pushcart Prize and the Million Writers Award. In 2012 his debut novel Zombie Attack! Rise of the Horde won Best Zombie/Horror E-book on Goodreads.

He currently lives in Venice Beach, California with his wife and dog.

I still get a lot of people that bring this story up to me. I've received my fair share of compliments on it since *Hobart* first ran it. It's funny, because at the time I just wanted to make the baseball issue of *Hobart* so badly that I wasn't thinking about what I was writing or how it would sound years later, but it still gets me every time I read it. It's all based on events in my own life around my adolescence, just scrambled around. It's a time capsule, a view into a world that no longer exists, and it makes me miss those days when everything was still exploding with possibility and the future was wide open. It reminds me of all the people I knew back then, especially him.

Julius was actually my great grandfather, but since my mom was very young when she had me, I got to know him as my grandfather growing up. He really was a pitcher and damn good too. In high school a scout had him pitch to Babe Ruth. True story. All he'd ever say is that he did well and we were all so impressed we never thought to ask more. Later he was drafted by the White Sox but broke his pitching arm and had to retire. He really did ride the rails and tell me about Hobo knowledge. He really did go into the cement industry after he settled in California. He really did have a heart attack walking home from the grocery store and thought it was just indigestion. He sat down for a while to catch his breath, then went home and went to bed. The next day he had a double bypass.

Julius was tough as nails, a survivor who never complained and worked hard all his life, and he really did give me my love of the game and the Dodgers. I think of him when I watch the games and know that if he were with me he'd be yelling along at the screen as well, cheering and cussing and applauding. I know he'd be proud to see how the Dodgers have been playing the last few years, just like he'd be proud to know I wrote a story about him that made it into a book.

This is for you Julius. I miss you.

*

Andrew Shuta (illustrations, pp. 28 & 102) is an artist and musician. He co-runs Spork Press and DJs weekly in Tucson.

*

Justin St. Germain ("A Phan's Notes: The Professional Ballplayer," p. 93) is the author of the memoir *Son of a Gun*, which won the 2013 Barnes & Noble Discover Prize and was named a best book of 2013 by Amazon, *Library Journal, Salon, Bookpage,* and *Publisher's Weekly*. He teaches at Oregon State University.

I wrote this piece the week leading up to the release of my first book. I'd been waiting a long time to see it in print, and this was the last of a series of short essays about baseball I pitched mostly to keep me from losing my mind in the meantime. I watched more than a hundred Phillies games that year, their first losing season in a decade. Two years later, they're in last place again, and, from what I can tell on the internet, Scott Hairston's out of baseball. I wish the Phillies would sign him.

*

Jill Talbot's ("Seams," p. 123) *The Way We Weren't: A Memoir* is out from Soft Skull Press in Summer 2015. Her work has appeared in *Brevity, DIAGRAM, Ecotone, The Normal School, The Paris Review Daily, Passages North, The Rumpus,* and more. Her website is jilltalbot.net.

This essay began with a moment: Ventura's rush to the mound and my hand on my father's arm in disbelief. I looked up the video on MLB. com and watched it again and again, amazed at how my memory of the moment challenged the evidence of it. I knew I wanted to write about that discrepancy, but I also knew I needed to go beyond and beneath it, to catalogue memories of my father and my grandfather—moments I only know through my father's telling, which resulted in a layering of memory—my father's, my recollection of his tellings, and my recreation of them in writing. That tripling of memory along with my father's, my grandfather's, and my own experiences with baseball created what I consider to be a braided essay.

*

James Yates ("Hands of Grace," p. 87) is an MFA Candidate in Creative Writing at Roosevelt University, and he serves as a contributing editor to Longform.org. His fiction has appeared in *Hobart, CHEAP POP, Pithead Chapel, Luna Luna Magazine,* and *WhiskeyPaper*. He lives in Chicago's Rogers Park neighborhood.

This was my first published story, and surprisingly, I don't hate it. I remember watching this game with my father: I didn't get into baseball until I was a teenager, and the entire '98 season was how we bonded during a tumultuous year (a death in the family, my awkward transition to high school/teen angst). Nostalgia has never been a major part of my adult life, but the memories of that game (Sosa's home runs, the back-and-forth score, Mark Grace's plays) have stayed with me: with each big play, I jumped on the couch like a maniac, and my father got teary-eyed when Sosa did his curtain calls.

As my writing and craft developed, I kept thinking about how to fictionalize that game, and I decided to reflect it through two lenses: one, with the attention on my favorite Cub; and two, from a fictional apartment in Chicago, where the atmosphere is decidedly less exhilarating than what I remember. At first, it was written as the grotesque opposite of me and my father: the drafts included a father shooting heroin while a little boy watched the game. This evolved into the failing relationship here: baseball is the source of and the filter of miscommunication, potential repressed attraction, and the overwhelming impossibility of verbalizing what is intangible. There were thousands of TVs tuned to that game; I'm sure not every living room was happy or caught up in the history.

*

Nicholas Ward's ("The First Game," p. 109) writing has appeared in *Post Road Magazine, Great Lakes Review, Eunoia Review, HYPERtext Magazine*, and the 2nd Story podcast, with whom he is a company member. He lives in Chicago with Fatimah, the poet, and Amadeus, the cat.

In 2009, I went to a Tigers game in Chicago against the White Sox. The second half of a doubleheader, it featured a recently flailing and washed up Jose Contreras absolutely flumox the Tigers over eight innings, allowing only one win and one walk. The game was neither exciting nor meaningful. However, a few months later the Tigers would blow a division lead they'd maintained all season and lose to the Minnesota Twins in a one-game playoff. If Contreras doesn't miraculously dominate them in the game I attended way back in June, do they win the division? The World Series? Probably not. But I like the idea of magnifying the game's seemingly insignificant individual moments, connecting them to my personal history, larger feelings of nostalgia, philosophy of the sport, and finally the place itself.

*

Terrance Wedin ("The Loneliness of the Designated Pinch Runner," p. 75) was born and raised in Blacksburg, Virginia. His work has appeared in *Esquire, The Rumpus, Barrelhouse, Fanzine*, and *Smartish Pace*.

I've always been fascinated by the unusual or unorthodox in baseball. As a kid, I was obsessed with players like Jim Abbott pitching with one hand, Craig Biggio starting a game at catcher and finishing at second base, or John Olerud playing first base while wearing a batting helmet. I don't know when I first heard about "the only" (this, like everything in baseball, is disputed...) designated pinch runner in MLB history, former college sprinter, Herb Washington, but I was instantly captivated by his most infamous moment as a player, which occurred during the 1974 World Series. The heartbreak and the humanity of such a moment! To fail at the specialized skill he was hired to do and on the world's biggest stage! To fail at it with two outs in the bottom of the ninth! In Herb Washington and that moment on first base versus the Dodgers, I saw a truth present, one that transcended the game of baseball. I don't know if Herb Washington was actually married by 1974. I don't know what hotel he stayed at or what his coach said to him, either. Maybe he took a bus to the stadium. Maybe he ate a continental breakfast that morning alone. I don't know. I made all that stuff up. I tried taking a moment of truth found in a play by play and attempted breathing some life into it by imagining what Herb might have been thinking before, during, and right after he got picked off by Mike Marshall. Really, I am in debt to Mr. Washington for being alive, for playing a game I love, for being part of history, and for taking that extra lead off first. Oakland would win the series in five games. Herb Washington would be released thirteen games into the next season, ending his short-lived baseball career. He would go on to have a successful career as a restauranteur, opening five McDonald's restaurants in the Rochester, New York area.

*

Claire Zulkey ("Take Me Out," p. 1) lives in Evanston, IL where she runs the very old blog Zulkey.com She is the author of the books for young people *An Off Year* and *Best Frenemies*.

Since I wrote my *Hobart* baseball piece a lot has happened: I moved twice, I got engaged, and then married, got a new job, published some books, had one son and am about to have another. And the White Sox won the World Series. Partially because of my own, busier life, and probably because the Sox did win a World Series, I don't follow them as closely as I once did. The players I knew and loved on the 2005 team have moved on and that mutual needing, of them for me to root for them, of me for them to do well, no longer exists. I still listen to and watch games when I remember they're on but I don't always remember they're on. I don't feel bad about this--it's just life. I will always be a White Sox fan and my son will always be named after Paul Konerko (my husband will protest that he was also named for some other people as well but for me it was largely after that dependable, hardworking, polite, non-flashy first baseman.) We may take our firstborn son to his first game this year. I anticipate that the noise might scare him and that we'll only stay for a few innings but with the experience I will be possibly be planting the seeds for a new relationship I have with the team. Hope still springs eternal.